Streetwise Spirituality

Streetwise Spirituality

28 Days to Inner Fitness

and

Everyday Enlightenment

Carol Marleigh Kline

NorLightsPress.com
2721 Tulip Tree Rd.
Nashville, IN 47448

Printed in the United States of America

Publisher's Cataloging-in-Publication Data
  (Provided by Quality Books, Inc.)

Kline, Carol Marleigh.
    Streetwise Spirituality : 28 days to inner fitness
    and everyday enlightenment / by Carol Marleigh Kline.
    p. cm.
Back cover author photo: Images by Floom

ISBN-13: 978-1-935254-26-3
First printing, 2010

1. Spiritual life.   I. Title.

BL624.K55 2009   204.4
QBI09-600228

CONTENTS

Acknowledgments

I want to thank Katherine Leonard, PhD, Nataliya Schetchikova, PhD, Sandy Jost, PhD, Betty Halley, RN, and Harriet Cohen Cooke, MD, for their critiques. I value their insights, suggestions, and questions.

I am particularly grateful to Ken Wilcox. Without his sleuthing after materials and years of evenings and weekends devoted to putting aging audiotapes on CDs, there would be no book.

Thanks to formatter Melody Culver. Gifted, supportive, and wise, Melody smoothed the process from beginning to end.

A special word of thanks to my literary agent, Krista Goering, and to my publishers, Sammie and Dee Justesen, for saying "Yes!"

Words cannot express the depth of my gratitude to the infinitely generous lecturer, the infinitely patient Mr. Tate, and my mother, who became the angel on my shoulder, just as she said she would.

Finally, although the stories are based on my life (except for *"Bungee Jumper"*), names have been changed and situations have been fictionalized to protect others' privacy.

Carol Marleigh Kline
Portland, Oregon
April 2010

Chapter One
The Secret

For eleven years, that battered brown box sat unopened in Japan. It crisscrossed America four times—still unopened. Parked forlornly on the floor of my new-to-me Oregon condo, it was out of place and out of time. With every move, I considered tossing it, but couldn't. Inside were keys to a life I might have led, a secret I had kept from almost everyone.

Looking at my watch, I pick up the scissors and slit the tape. I shuffle through hundreds of lecture transcripts, the papers dotted with mildew. *"Ten minutes,"* I say aloud. That's all it will take to skim through these pages and shove them into a garbage bag. The minutes become hours. The bag remains empty. In flashbacks, I recall the strong voice of the lecturer as he speaks of life, death, and everything in between. *"We think our experiences come to us by chance,"* he says. *"Chance doesn't exist. You can get hit by a car while crossing the street because your mind is somewhere else. That's not chance. It has a cause—your carelessness. It has an effect—your early and quite unnecessary death."*

Physical pain, he said, means the body needs care. If the emotions are stirred, however, Earth School is in session. Heart and mind are calling on us to search our inner currents and make better choices than in the past. That search, he said, can lead to spiritual growth and understanding.

The lecturer outlined a set of life skills meant to help us meet our everyday challenges. Practical to the core, the skills were useful when we felt frustrated to the breaking point or when we felt afraid or rejected. They were comforting after deep loss. They helped explain why love that felt so good could feel so bad. If we mastered them, he said, we would no longer find ourselves running blindly through our days, wondering what was going on, and hoping to dodge all the bullets but the last one.

"We are in Earth School to grow past personality and biological drives, past what we've been taught, past social and cultural expectations," he said. *"We are here to deepen our connections to our*

innermost selves and to each other."

The lecturer touted no new religion. There was no one to worship and nothing to take on faith. Happiness and inner peace were not goals, but by-products of daily practice of the life skills. Enlightenment, he said, came about when people put heart and soul into building inner fitness. Enlightened people had one basic textbook—life. The more we used these life skills, the more we would positively affect the world as a whole, just as every wave in the ocean is connected to every other wave. The concept was generous and I liked it well enough, but I was only 13 when I first heard those lectures. They ran late, often on school nights. My attention wavered and my bed called to me.

Back then, I never asked myself what I was doing on this planet. When my mother found what she called a "practical spirituality," though, I caught her excitement. We joined some 200 people who gathered twice weekly in Los Angeles to listen to talks that made sense even to the child-woman that I was. Originally from Egypt, the lecturer taught there for 35 years. He never made a dime for what he did. Why isn't his name in this book? *"Only the teachings count,"* he said. *"My name is unimportant."*

I was just 17 when I rejected all thought of inner growth. I did not want to believe that anything I did made a difference. My friends weren't talking about purpose. They cared about fun. I cared about what they cared about, and I was passionately determined to fit in. I was not going to blaze any trails, spiritual or otherwise. Still, I continued to add copies of the lectures to that box for years, wanting reminders of a time when even the most ordinary event took on extraordinary meaning.

Traces of mud are still on my boots. I can talk from the shadow side. I am definitely no angel. Knowing the person I was, I can't imagine I would have done things any differently. In these pages, you will see what one flawed person did to turn life around—when I rediscovered and put to use the wisdom found in a stack of dumpster-bound transcripts.

Chapter Two
Dreamchaser

I was a gangly, knobby-kneed girl who grew very tall very fast. At nearly 6 feet, I was a lonely loner with no idea what to make of life, so I looked to Hollywood for answers. American movies promised men a good life if they worked hard and made money. Women had to be beautiful. And *nice*. Hollywood bitches never kept what little happiness they found. My last guideline came from the *Great Book of Women's Wisdom: "When in pain, eat chocolate."*

Most of all, I was desperate to fall in love and to remain in that state of blessed insanity forever. Beginning in my teens, though, love was always the same. The first weeks were thrilling, followed by the fading of that Fourth-of-July feeling. And wasn't true love measured by the fireworks in a lover's kiss?

I was 20 when the movies set me on a career path. On Saturday nights, my boyfriend and I watched samurai movies at the local theater. Screen samurai took mortal offense at insults that seemed not worth drawing your sword over. They turned their backs on what I most wanted: Security. Infinitely layered, unwritten social rules kept everyone tightly wound. Nonconformists had no place in Japan, but the Japanese respected writers—who were nonconformists. Nothing about being Japanese was simple.

As hard as I tried to fit into my own culture, I could not crack the code. I smiled a lot. Tried not to take up too much space. Rarely expressed an opinion. Kept my emotions to myself lest they carry me somewhere I did not want to go. Japan gave me an out. If I could not be American apple pie, I could try for American sushi. Sad-eyed, kimono-clad people whose hearts bled into exquisite lines of poetry made me weep. My curiosity was aroused by, among other things, the bow. You bowed low for some people, and not so low for others. How did anyone figure it out?

Perplexed and magnetized by questions trivial and deep, I set sail
for the life of a college teacher with a specialty in things Japanese. My
choice was eccentric, but eccentricity was fine in my culture if you could
make a living at it. This ambition determined every move I made for
seven years.

From the University of Southern California, I headed for New
York and Columbia University's East Asian Studies department. Like
everyone else, I was on a year-to-year fellowship. Fearful of losing it, I
pared my life down to nothing but books. Well, almost.

Every six weeks or so, I allowed the Metropolitan Opera to make
passionate, safe love to my dried-up scholar's heart. At midnight, exalted
and exhausted, I stumbled out onto the street to take the subway back
to my fifth-floor walkup. While I lived in New York, my emotional life
began and ended with opera.

Three years later, I flew to the former Stanford Center in Tokyo to
study Japanese while writing a Master's thesis. When my fellowship
there vanished overnight, I stayed in Japan—too stubborn to go home.
Eighteen months later, my remaining academic dreams crumbled,
leaving me with no particular reason to get up in the morning. Like so
many Westerners there, I taught English conversation to achieve my two
remaining life goals: Eating and paying the rent. Later, I became a Tokyo
newscaster and talk show host. My husband-to-be and I met when my
best friend, his wife, was about to leave him. More on that story, and on
the derailed dreams, later.

On my eleventh anniversary in Japan, a yearning to go home while
America still felt like home put me on a plane to Los Angeles. What I
didn't know was that American TV stations ranked themselves from #1
to about #200—and foreign TV stardom counted for nothing. Frustrated,
I took broadcast journalism courses at U.S.C., looking for a way in. For
a year, Stu flew to L.A. every three months, stayed a day or two, and
headed back to Tokyo.

To blunt the edge of pain and loneliness, I'd flip on the set to catch
the news—and wind up watching nonstop until my eyelids slid south.
As long as the TV was on, lively adventures and handsome men were
mine. By morning, the images had faded and the hunt was on again for
something to fill all the holes in my life.

Finally, I asked my commuter husband for a divorce. In six weeks,
he had moved to Los Angeles. From there, we drove 3,000 miles to

my new job as a TV reporter in High Point, North Carolina. People at the television station packed exciting or numbing activities into every waking moment. I did, too. There were parties, wine, and relationships. We chased endlessly after everything new. All of us lived as if boredom were a capital crime.

In time, I discovered that jobs you love can go away and marriages can blow apart. And chocolate? Chocolate takes you only so far. If picks and shovels dig gold out of a mine, I wondered, what tools do people have to dig *life* out of life?

I looked for a quick fix in my favorite bookstore's personal growth section. One author recommended gratitude—another touted love. Seeing no evidence that these authors' feet even touched the ground, I could not relate. Why should I be grateful for pain? How could I love those I didn't even like? Shelves of inspiring books gathered dust in my house—all read and forgotten, along with notes taken at too many instant life-transformation workshops.

If, as my society told me, happiness for a woman meant having a good man, a good job, and maybe a pair of fabulous shoes, life would never be more than the sunlit flash off a bluebird's wings. I was determined that my last words would not be, *"Is that all there is?"*

My days were a sideways slide through time. I watched as people spoiled the present by clinging to the past. Others, like me, struggled to achieve a dream, only to throw it away in a moment of recklessness.

A few managed to be at home in their own skins. They laughed often—with people, not at them. Neither doormats nor saints, they were several cuts above me as I drifted along, seeking to find love and avoid pain. They might suffer, but they didn't ask, *"Why me?"* These people had to be faking it, I decided. What were they like when no one was watching? Wasn't it exhausting to pretend to be so above it all, so ready to roll with everything life threw at them? I knew how hard it was to live a lie. Here I was, years into trying to manufacture a permanent persona I could stand. Still trying my best to be someone I wasn't.

Chapter Three
Earth School: If Not Now

Still surrounded by piles of musty transcripts, I read these words: *"Your lives are short, no matter how long they are."* At 17, my best years had been ahead of me. No talk about time limits or life missions was going to slow me down then. Maybe I'd get serious later. Well, "later" had arrived and all I could think was, *"If not now, when?"*

A School Like No Other

The lecturer insisted that no matter what it looks like, life is not a random series of events. Earth School, he said, has its own ABCs. They are: a) learn, b) grow, and c) expand in consciousness. Each experience moves us into the path of learning opportunities. In Earth School, nobody gets "social promotions." Tests are cheat-proof. And we can't call in sick. Sleeping through class only puts off the inevitable—the lessons that are ours to learn.

"So, if this is a school," I thought, *"why haven't I seen it from day one?"* That's easy, the lecturer said. The drama blinds us to what's going on. Life lessons are subtle, complex, enthralling, or devastating. They distract us. We don't see how exquisitely custom-designed they are. *"Maybe so,"* I thought, *"but show me."*

Two days later, I found my answer in a transcript: *"Earth School lies in our repetitive patterns. Do we repeatedly attract romantic partners who can't commit? Are close friends demanding or selfish? Do we pitch our tents on the edge of burnout?"* Repetitive patterns, the lecturer said, are guideposts to what we have not yet mastered. If gold lay buried in my repetitive patterns, I thought, I was a wealthy woman.

Whatever the experience, he told us, our attitude determined its quality. We could always make a bad experience better—or worse.

Getting to the Good Things

Many cultures, the lecturer told us, don't value what's most important in Earth School—the little stuff. Like how to create peace of mind in the midst of chaos. Like how to uncover moments of happiness in completely unexpected places. Like how to love and be loved. We rarely get around to putting the little things where they belong—at the center of our lives. It's not that we can't have the good things in life that aren't free, he said. We can. But they aren't why we're here.

Where the Pitfalls Are

Even those who take an evolutionary slow boat, he told us, still get where they're going. Later, if not sooner. If we think sooner is better than later, it's possible to pick up the pace. All it takes is the willingness to think for ourselves. That's where I drew the line. Nobody tells *me* what to think.

Consider this, he said: If we believe we create our assumptions and attitudes, our biases and preferences all by ourselves, we're mistaken. We pick up ideas with the very air we breathe, from friends and family, through what we hear and see, and in how we react to pain and loss. The longer we hold on to these ideas, the more fixed they become. Like boxes we haven't opened in a decade, ideas benefit from a periodic airing out.

Okay, so where was I supposed to find worn-out ideas that no longer served me? In our reactions, he said. When we get upset because someone else takes "our" parking space. When someone decides to stop loving us. When we share a holiday with the family and all the same fights are fought again with all the same people for all the same reasons. When we feel irritated over having to do what we don't want to do. Getting upset doesn't change reality, he said. It doesn't make things better. Chances are, it makes them worse. We know that, but we vent our emotions anyway. We think the world should know that we don't like having to deal with change. *"Do we know anyone on Earth who escapes change?"* he asked.

I had a short fuse that was easily lit when I felt unfairly treated, or even when I just bashed my toe against a pile of books I'd left on the floor. Wasn't it normal to feel a fire in the belly at such times—and let it roar? It was perfectly normal for someone who operated on automatic, he said. But if I wanted to move on up the ladder in Earth School, to evolve past the familiar emotional smog, I would have to start looking at things in a new way. That idea did not please me, but the lecturer said that Earth School is not designed to please anyone. Instead, it's all about learning. If we're still walking around in Earth School, he added, we still have lessons to learn. By learning them, we move on to the next level, and the next. That's where the really good stuff is—but getting there requires some internal housecleaning.

Chapter Four

Earth School: Outer Mind and Soul Mind

A program so complex that it provides exactly the right life lessons for each human being from birth through death is beyond my power to imagine, but that's Earth School, said the lecturer. Who, then, are the architects, the teachers behind our multidimensional mosaic of a classroom? Who lays out the endlessly interrelated opportunities for us to respond in a more enlightened way? Life would be simpler if those who have already figured things out were still around—if we had an army of Earth School "graduates" to answer our questions. We don't. So you and I still sit in our child-sized seats, knees poking out into the aisles. Now and then, we glimpse what we're here for. More often, we miss the cues. Or we just coast.

Even though we can't see our two primary teachers, we know one of them intimately. It's what we call "the voice in our heads." If we pay attention to its gabble, said the lecturer, we'll notice that none of it takes us anywhere new. Those erratic thought patterns are very different from the creative daydream flow—daydreams known to inventors and artists. That flow accesses our second teacher, soul mind.

Each of these two teachers has its own way of acting and its own goals. One dies when we do. The other does not. The teacher who dies (the voice in our heads) is closely tied to material things, to competition, and to fear. Most people's lives, said the lecturer, don't get much beyond this level. That grumpy, self-satisfied teacher encourages us to react out of unthinking habit.* It tempts us to forget what we're here for— the learning, the growing, and the expansion of consciousness. Playing on our emotions, it keeps us under its thumb by pumping up our fears, our doubts, and our many hungers. We cannot grow much as long as it's

---

*Gary Zukav, author of Seat of the Soul, calls a reaction a choice rooted in habit, while a response is creative, healthy, and made in the moment. That same distinction is respectfully made throughout *Streetwise Spirituality*.

in charge. And only conscious choices, made consistently, can train that teacher to shift direction over time.

Something this important needs a name. The difficulty with terms like "ego," "egoic mind," and "personality" is the baggage they carry. Psychologists put a positive spin on the ego. To them, it's our identity. People on the street don't agree. To us, it's an overinflated sense of self-worth. The word "personality" is equally murky.

Here we'll call the disgruntled Earth School teacher "outer mind." Outer mind is with us all of our lives, and the havoc it creates is almost inconceivable.

Meet Outer Mind

We can temporarily drown out the voice of the outer mind. We all know how. A glass of wine. A shopping trip. Blanked-out hours with something electronic. At the end of the day, though, we are still alone with ourselves—and with that voice. Outer mind, however, is not some great cosmic error. It has its purpose. We could not survive in Earth School without it. Outer mind helps us navigate through the mazes of this material life. It focuses on keeping us alive. To learn our lessons, the lecturer reminded us, a body is required. Outer mind tells us not to step in front of speeding cars. It reminds us to eat. It urges us to do what it takes to keep the species going.

Outer mind gets out of hand, though, when it tries to run our lives through its infantile emotions and its utter disdain for logic. When we become frightened, insulted, disappointed, or defeated, outer mind pushes us to react as we always have. Why pause to analyze what's going on? The outer mind is always right, right? Maybe we have a habit of shouting foul words at other drivers from the safety of our car—windows rolled up, of course. Outer mind croons, *"Go for it."*

Outer Mind in Charge

The Earth-bound outer mind nags and yammers. It uses any tactic to create negative beliefs that keep it in control. It lies to us and never looks back. It stokes the fires of fantasy. It sucks hard on past pain. It reinforces our conditioning, our stereotypes, and our memories. It wants what it wants when it wants it. Outer mind honks and shouts: *"Me first!"* It manipulates people and considers their suffering only a means to an end. The negative belief at work is, *"My needs are paramount. I am free to do whatever it takes to get them met."*

Outer mind may choose bigotry to feel superior. It can't stand to be contradicted because only one side of any issue could possibly exist— its side. Outer mind likes to steal good ideas—*"Why give credit where credit is due?"* Notice how often outer mind leaps up to blame others for bad situations we've brought on ourselves. When things go well, see how quickly it says, *"Thanks to me! All thanks to me!"*

Stories it tells about other people show them in a lesser light. Outer mind loves being the star. The negative belief is: *"I must show everyone how special I am."* Outer mind takes no joy in other people's successes. *"She wouldn't have won that race if I'd had a good night's sleep."* Outer mind has a half-dozen forgotten projects around the house. It drops projects—and relationships—when the novelty wears off: *"Boring!"*

Outer mind can also rule us by generating feelings of inferiority. *"Everyone else is better/smarter/more spiritually evolved than I am."* *"I'm hopeless." "I have no control over my addiction to food/sex/alcohol/ drugs."*

Outer mind's hungers are very young and insatiable. Outer mind tempts us to give in to cravings because addictions make people feel out of control, keeping outer mind in control. Outer mind is all about power and the belief that everyone on Earth is either inferior or superior to everyone else. The lecturer said the outer mind likes comparisons. It may see others as material or mental pygmies, compared to us. When the outer mind is in the driver's seat, we say, *"I am greater." "I have more." "I am recognized and you are not."*

Those who see themselves as inferior feel invisible and weak. They may spend their lives trying to fill others' needs out of a desire to feel worthwhile. But they can never do enough to bring themselves peace. That's because they are using the tools of outer mind to manipulate others' passions or thoughts—a strategy that cannot bring about inner peace or wholeness.

The outer mind presents the greatest challenges that any of us will ever face. The lecturer said that if we allow its signature markers such as selfishness, despair, judgment, or ingratitude to run us, outer mind will succeed in distracting us from the great work at hand. It will keep us from evolving. We will stay locked in place until we are brought to our knees.

With outer mind in the driver's seat, we can become cynical, seeing a self-centered agenda behind any kind act. We may become disillusioned, calling happy people fools. Alienated, and in thrall to outer mind, we may say, *"Ah, the world is no damned good."*

The lecturer said that every trouble on Earth is created by the outer mind. *"Some may call that mind the 'devil,"* he added. *"It's the only devil that any of us will ever know. The outer mind wants nothing more than to rule, dictate, and destroy what's standing in its way—when it isn't busy satisfying one of its infinite hungers or whims."* The outer mind tears us apart in its passion for dominance. It feeds on our chemistry, DNA, upbringing, past experiences, and dark emotions.

If we spend all our days in getting and spending, in loving, losing, and blaming, or in fighting or ignoring our lessons, the lecturer told us, fresh opportunities arrive to become more conscious and true to our deepest selves. Why are we attracted to the wrong people? We are not fools. We don't want to love them. It's only a dance of two souls, both with something to teach, both with something to learn. Many of our most important lessons are brought to us through difficult relationships.

We may hope that if we ignore our purpose long enough, it will go away. It won't. Why we're here is rooted in who we are. We can't get rid of who we are, so that brings us full circle, right back to what we didn't want to face to begin with.

We may get upset when we don't have what we expect. We may say, *"I deserve better!"* Why? Do we think that physical beauty, education, money, status, or some other external measuring stick should determine our quality of life? Are we blind to everything but our pleasures or making a living? *"We call this human nature,"* said the lecturer. *"If it is, it holds us close to Earth and keeps us from growing spiritually."*

Many people make the mistake of thinking that the outer mind, together with its beliefs and prejudices and baggage, is who they are, and all that they are. Unaware of why they are here, they stagnate.

The outer mind focuses on externals. It tells us, *"Seeing is believing."* Seeing is not believing, the lecturer said. The eye deceives us. The five senses are *"lovely liars,"* he said. *"They tell us that what we see, hear, smell, touch, or taste is more important than what we feel and know at a deep level."* The five senses help us function in the outside world. But if we let them, the senses can distract us from who we are by stimulating and feeding the energies of the outer mind.

Outer Mind's Higher Purpose

The outer mind has a higher purpose. Outer mind is designed to eventually enrich itself through learning, and to apply that learning to our growing understanding, the lecturer told us. Day by day, we can improve our lives, pay our karma, and interact with each other in ways that show we are more than sleepwalking members of this species—that we are evolving.

Meet Soul Mind

Our eyes tell us we are forever separate, said the lecturer, but our hearts know we are forever connected. The heart connection is made through the soul. The soul is the individualized portion of the oneness in each of us. The soul communicates with us through soul mind, which is our other internal teacher, the only part of us that is eternal.

Conscience, Common Sense, and Intuition

Soul mind uses conscience, common sense, and intuition to guide us toward growth and learning.

Conscience is one of soul mind's most recognizable voices, he said. When we are tempted by outer mind to do something that will hurt us or someone else, it's conscience that advises us to choose otherwise.

Common sense helps us respond to life in practical, reasonable ways based on reality, not fantasy.

Intuition is another soul mind voice. The outer mind tries to dismiss soul mind's hunches as figments of our imagination. We may act on our intuition—and a hunch may turn out to be right—but our doubting outer mind will say, *"That's a coincidence. Since when are you psychic?"*

Soul mind constantly tries to warn us through impressions, premonitions, and hunches. If we listen, we leave the door open to receive more such gifts. Hunches and impressions make us aware of what is coming, often as a result of poor choices we made in the past. We may not remember what we did long ago, but soul mind's memory is 20/20, the lecturer told us.

Paying Karma

In Earth School, soul mind custom designs the basic curriculum— our life lessons. And it is soul mind that judges our actions, thoughts, words, and feelings. If the soul believes that suffering will help us learn a lesson, we will suffer, but suffering is only a potential teaching tool and its value lies in how we use it. The purpose is not to punish, but to teach. Soul mind works toward balancing the ledger while we pay off the karma we've brought on ourselves. *"Karma? I've done nothing to bring on bad karma,"* we may say. *"Why should I have such a hard life?"* Soul mind takes the long view. How could anyone learn all there is to learn in a single incarnation? Even if we wanted to, we could not. And most of us don't really want to. We'd rather wait for others to change first. *"If he starts being more loving toward me, I'll be more loving toward him."* With that mindset, we can miss the changes that would take place in our lives if we became the kind of person we want others to be, of loving in the way that we wish we were loved.

When I went to parties in my teens and twenties, I sat off by my introverted self, danced when asked, and used my little set speech: *"This is a really nice home, isn't it? They've painted the walls pretty colors."* I said the same boring thing to each partner. After I'd said "the words," I went mute. Dancing with me was as stimulating as wrapping your arms around a broom. I never thought to ask a man about his interests. To me, finding love was all chance. It was supposed to be pure chemistry, all myth and magic. Prince Charming would see through my quiet disguise. I had so very much to learn.

The Blueprint

Some people believe everything is pre-destined, but the lecturer says no. Certain experiences are laid out in advance by soul mind—people to meet, challenges to overcome, and joys to delight in—but we make of them what we will and a passive approach to life gets us nowhere. How can we grow if we roll over and play dead?

Taking Charge

The lecturer told us that each moment is the most important moment of our lives. That's because soul mind and our lessons are in the now, but outer mind focuses on past history and future fantasies.

In one moment, the soul mind may bring us a visit from a difficult relative, the loss of a crucial document, a family struggle over a will, or the temptation to do something we will later regret. Soul mind is not "leading us into evil." It's giving us an opportunity to choose between reacting as we typically do, or responding in a more spiritually mature manner. Soul mind asks us to take charge, to stay awake to all opportunities. We can only arise or awaken by changing our attitudes and our behaviors, and by applying toward others the truths we discover.

All Prayers Answered

Many ask why their prayers aren't answered. Prayers, said the lecturer, are always answered, but not necessarily in the way we think they should be. This is where those ABCs come in. How would we mature spiritually if soul mind beat up all the playground bullies for us? We wouldn't, so it doesn't. Soul mind encourages our growth. It does not interfere with that process.

Where Hope Lives

Soul mind, he said, is perfect. It's our "better angel." It needs no development. Instead, we develop the outer mind through more conscious responses to life. The outer mind absorbs spiritual lessons, not soul mind. Spiritual lessons are crucial to the outer mind so it can grow and expand in understanding. The more we learn, grow, and expand in consciousness, the more the soul mind can unfold, awaken, and express through us, the lecturer said.

As that process continues, what we think of as "us" begins to expand through a deepening connection to soul mind. For "no reason" we may call a friend and that call may change or even save a life. Soul mind waits for us to make better choices over time. At our deepest level, we hunger to know soul mind. Soul mind, said the lecturer, brings hope to the desperate or despairing heart.

Listening for Soul Mind

If we want to connect with soul mind, we must invite it to the table. The language it uses is gentle. Some people ask why soul mind doesn't speak up, why it isn't as insistent as outer mind. Outer mind is rooted in the physical, the lecturer explained, while soul mind is rooted in the spiritual. We see the physical, but we sense the spiritual. Physicality and spirituality reside in different dimensions, so they abide by different rules.

Soul mind does try to get our attention. It blends into our thinking processes, wanting to connect. Unless we're looking for it to show up, though, we may not notice. Soul mind wants to take the lead as much as outer mind does. It will not, however, push outer mind aside. Soul mind must be patiently, consistently asked to step forward.

If we're consciously looking for it, we can find soul mind all around us. Wisdom is a soul mind attribute, as are peace, love, gratitude, kindness, and compassion. Those who treat everyone with respect are responding to soul mind. People who handle what comes their way with patience are feeling the soul mind's pull.

Creativity is another soul mind attribute. When we are riding the flow of our deeper creativity, we know peace, and we know soul mind. When a totally unexpected solution comes up for a problem we've been grappling with, we have soul mind to thank for it.

Life improves as we catch hold of the rising spiral of inner growth that comes from working in concert with soul mind. The more we choose soul mind's options, the more we build inner fitness. The more internally fit we become, the lecturer said, the more soul mind is able to work with us. On the other hand, the more we give in to outer mind's momentary whims, the harder it is to hear what soul mind has to say.

Nothing Lost

All that we say, do, think, or feel is recorded. We may wish we could sweep some of our past under the cosmic rug, but nothing is ever lost. How could anything be left out or erased when soul mind, and no one else, weighs our responses to life, judges our actions and our motivations, and decides what is to come? To leave something out would be unfair, and that is not soul mind's way. The God within is a just and loving God, the lecturer told us. Soul mind is always in our corner. Soul mind keeps hoping that we will take the better path at the next fork in the road.

Outer Mind and Soul Mind: The Continuum

When we weigh outer mind and soul mind, it would be easy to assume that one is "bad" and the other "good." After all, life on Earth is based on dualities—black and white, push and pull, positive and negative, male and female. So why not "bad" and "good" for these aspects of mind?

If everything is ultimately one, and it is, the two must meet somewhere. They cannot remain forever separate. Picture them like this:

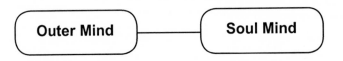

As you see, they are on a continuum. Outer mind resonates more to Earthly interests. Soul mind resonates more to non-Earthly concerns. We'd get into a lot less trouble if outer mind weren't around, but we could not learn what we are here to learn without it. It presents challenges for us to overcome so that we can grow toward a healthier, more spiritual outlook. Outer mind exists to be worked with, not despised. We all struggle with it. It's a tool for growth—neither more nor less.

We are free to respond to our experiences from soul mind's book or to react to life from outer mind's book. We do this all the time. Every day. That's really all we do in Earth School. We may dislike the situations we are presented with, or we may be ecstatically happy about them. That's not the point, said the lecturer. The point is, what can we learn from them? How can we grow? What can we share with others? How can we overcome what overcame us in the past? Finding answers to such questions helps us expand in consciousness.

Outer mind is like skin color. It can't be wished away or washed away. We're not here to ignore, cut off, or crush it. We're to train it to align with soul mind by making more evolved choices. Instead of just defending its territory, the lecturer explained, outer mind can change.

If we were working with a large, intelligent, willful dog, training would not be completed overnight—or if we worked at it only for five minutes every other Tuesday. With patient, consistent, daily effort and a willingness to bend, outer mind will grow. It will come to use its narrow focus on our individual Earth-rooted lives in a positive way— complementing soul mind's focus on life's big picture.

The outer mind may get irritated when someone refuses to help us or when we don't get the raise we think we deserve. We can, however, train outer mind not to blame or complain, but to look for soul mind's wisdom. When we do that, we open ourselves to other possibilities and other solutions—or simply to acceptance of reality. Outer mind can learn to deal with difficult or painful situations in a rational, intelligent way. The lecturer said that only after the outer mind begins to regularly give over to soul mind do we know true peace and freedom.

Will Power

We may wonder where will power comes into the picture. We can use our will to lose weight or learn a foreign language but it's true purpose is to guide outer mind to grow in the service of soul mind, the lecturer told us. This work becomes easier with time, but it's not a once-and-done proposition. We can never quite take our eyes off outer mind. It will slip its leash if given half a chance. An unruly outer mind is eager to fill any vacuum. That's why we find its babble in our brains when we first pursue peace on a meditation cushion.

People who merely "motivate" through their days—pursuing pleasure and avoiding pain—lead ordinary, unfocused lives, he added. Our lives only work well when we use the will to put soul mind in charge of both outer mind and the body. That is the natural order of things. Otherwise, the all-powerful outer mind uses the body to satisfy its momentary whims, with spirit as an afterthought.

It would be helpful, he said, to reverse that approach. He suggested that we ask spirit to illuminate and guide the mind and ask the body to do spirit's bidding while we carry out our daily tasks. Ongoing communication with soul mind cannot happen, he added, as long as outer mind runs the show. And every ounce of outer mind's energy is devoted to staying in power.

Balancing Mind, Body, and Spirit

Life begins to really work when we balance the three segments of life—mind, body, and spirit. To do that, we start where we are. If, for example, my life is 90% material and 10% spiritual, I will feel positive change with even a 5% increase in spiritual pursuits and awareness. Perhaps later, I'll feel drawn toward an 80/20 split, and so on.

We hurt ourselves mentally, physically, or spiritually, the lecturer said, only when we go overboard in one direction or the other. We may think we should give up every material comfort and abandon the world of relationships to live a "spiritual life." People who do that can become fanatics, just as overly materialistic people lose balance in the other direction. The lecturer did not measure spirituality by a materialistic yardstick. The rich are not less spiritual than the poor because they live in big houses and drive expensive cars, he said. The poor are not more spiritual because they have no money. As long as we are not possessed by our possessions, we are free to enjoy them. And as long as we do not hurt others or ourselves in the process of enjoying life, there's nothing wrong with having fun—quite the contrary.

Instant Transformation

Some people do undergo an amazing thunderbolt transformation from a life that resonates mainly to outer mind's many Earth-bound anchors to a life that spiritually soars. Suddenly, they understand. They are forever changed, lifted above the turmoil of everyday living. Such people may shine with soul mind's divine light and offer an inspirational beacon to the rest of us.

We can break our hearts, though, if we think that the only way to become enlightened is through a sudden, complete, and world-shattering illumination. Most of us move toward enlightenment one step at a time. As human beings, we'd all love to have instant change when we feel ready for it. We'd like to start out by soaring. But, the lecturer reminded us, first we crawl and then we walk. Soaring comes later.

Deep Connection

The lecturer explained that when we leave the door between the two teachers ajar, soul mind strives to envelop the outer mind, to teach and inspire. Meditation is the vehicle we use to give soul mind an opportunity to connect with outer mind. At the beginning of a meditation, we may want to encourage this process by saying to outer mind, *"Listen carefully. Listen and learn."*

"Soul mind," said the lecturer, *"wants to reveal what's good for us in this life. It wants to take our hand and walk with us along our life path. It is saying, 'Be still and know I am present. Be still and know I am here.' Never are you alone."*

Chapter Five
Earth School: Bridging Heart and Mind

*E*motions were a mystery to me from my earliest years. I was happy to be bound by love in ways that I wanted to be bound. I was glad to feel my heart swell with pride or fill with awe. Even sorrow could lead to a deeper understanding, a heartfelt connection. But other emotions made me want what I should not want, made me grieve the past, or yearn for what I could never have. What good was any of that?

Some people (and I was one of them) had no wish to be tossed rudderless on an ocean of emotion, so we mostly kept our feelings under lock and key. No matter how hard we battened down the hatches, though, sudden jailbreaks were not unknown. These were followed by even greater efforts to keep our cool. Living mostly in our heads, we missed out on much of what it meant to be fully human.

If I accepted the lecturer's statement that there are no mistakes in Earth School, emotions had to have a purpose beyond the ability to turn life on its head. I dug through the transcripts over and over, looking for ways emotions could be used for self-discovery and growth. Could emotions be used to build the inner peace they so often destroyed? Searching for answers, I set out on this part of the journey by examining the past—anyone's past.

We were born tiny scraps of human flesh that wanted only one thing: Control. We went from being automatically fed 24 hours a day to a "feeding schedule." From floating pleasantly in a 98.6-degree private pool, we were yanked into a too-noisy, too-bright place that was unpredictably hot, cold, wet, dry, soft, or hard. Alone and hungry and unable to speak our caregivers' language or go raid the refrigerator, we cried. If no one came, we screamed. If someone fed us, we learned that screaming was useful. If someone beat us, instead, we developed other control strategies. Perhaps we learned to smile and be "good babies." If we survived, we remembered what worked.

Emotions can range all the way from operatic to microscopic. If our caregivers are colorful screamers, we may copy them. If they hold back, we learn to pull a tight smile and say we're *"fine, just fine."* Most of us live somewhere between the two extremes—except when something unexpected happens. We may then react on autopilot—sometimes way out of proportion. Think, for example, of the man on the beltway in northern Virginia. Someone cuts in front of him. He guns his motor, weaving recklessly in and out of rush-hour traffic, intent on crashing into the other driver's car. You and I would never do that, would we?

Let's take a closer look at an emotion—maybe anger?—and at several reactions typical of Earth School.

- We may react on automatic and explode with rage like the man on the beltway. And learn nothing.
- We may swallow our anger. No learning here.
- We may blame, as in, *"You made me cry. It's all your fault. If you hadn't done X, I wouldn't have done Y."* By blaming someone else, we can avoid the lesson.
- We may numb out with TV, food, booze, drugs, or whatever. We think if we ignore dark emotions, they'll go away. They don't. They re-ignite when we feel challenged or frightened. When we distract ourselves, we postpone learning.
- We may go for a run or count to ten. Those are conscious strategies if they keep emotions in check while we connect heart and mind. If they are just numb-outs, again, we learn nothing.
- Creative people may transmute their anger into art, music, or literature. That's wonderful for the rest of us, but it doesn't let them off the hook. If artists don't examine and make use of their emotions, they stay stuck. Just like the rest of us.

Working with the "Shoulds"

How can we shift from painful or frightening emotions to feelings that lead to freedom, inner peace, and power? How do we make those feelings the foundation of everyday enlightenment?

Let me ask you a question. What ruins a perfectly good day for you? For me, it was any situation that brought up irritation, frustration, or stress. I knew that no wicked witch had handed me the glorious gift of anger on my 21st birthday. My daily life had been filled ever since I could remember with irritations and upsets, resentments, complaints, and the desire to point out others' errors. None of this was working for me as an adult. As little as I wanted to admit it, the child I had been was still sitting in the driver's seat. That child's vision was narrow and skewed. Nothing existed beyond the tip of her own nose. If I didn't re-evaluate my emotions and the fears that fueled them, how would anything change?

We no longer fear what made us cry as children. We aren't afraid of the bogeyman, loud noises, or the dark. We aren't afraid of people who are bigger than we are. If we don't examine our deeper fears, however, we give control of our lives to a child who has neither judgment nor wisdom—a child much like the outer mind. That child doesn't know the difference between fear of the dark and fear of dying alone—it's all fear. Small children don't have options. Adults do. If we forget that, we lose touch with the creativity that can teach us to live a life unbounded, instead of one that's hemmed in by fears expressed in our "shoulds." Connecting with soul mind and its values makes all the difference.

What are the "shoulds" that unconsciously move us? A husband may think, *"My wife should never keep me waiting."* He sits outside, rhythmically honking the horn and letting the whole neighborhood know that his wife is out of his control. A wife may think, *"If my husband really loved me, he'd turn off the game and talk to me."* Her fear is that he loves his diversions more than he loves her, so he's out of her control. Because we don't always do what others want us to do, we're not always on time, and we do get caught up in our habits and our addictions, dark emotions are a constant part of everyday life here in Earth School. If these emotions are not looked at consciously, they keep us prisoners in our own castles—forever honking our horns or feeling unloved.

We may weep or pound pillows. But nothing changes until we bravely walk past the smokescreen that emotions are to confront the real dragons—beliefs and attitudes rooted in the fear of being fundamentally helpless in the face of accidents, diseases, disasters, and other people's passions, peculiarities, and perversities.

The more that I come from fear, the further I slide into fear. My fears feed on unexamined shadows. While fears grow fat, my life grows thin.

By living unconsciously, our choices move toward self-protection, isolation, and deeper, darker fears. That suits outer mind just fine. It likes to be alone with us. When there's a choice between acting out of fear or love, outer mind elbows forward, whispering, *"Choose me!"*

When we are torn apart by our emotions, it feels like they are us, but we are much more than our passions. More than the agony that follows loss. More than our petty upsets. More than the payback anger that slips out as a snotty joke.

What else underlies our sadness, irritation, stress, frustration, depression, or outright anger? Why do we get upset when friends or lovers break dates with us? Because they should never disappoint us. But they do. Why does it make us mad when the neighbor's party goes on full blast until 2 a.m.? Because people should be considerate of our sleep schedules. They aren't. Why do we get upset when we can't fit into last summer's jeans? Because we should be able to eat anything we want and never gain weight. But we can't. We can't control others. We can't always even control ourselves, so do any of these "shoulds" make sense? No. Is that the way life works? No. Is that the way life has ever worked? No. So why do we cling to our false beliefs? We cling to them out of fear.

The "shoulds" give us what we think of as a solid, dependable raft on the shifting sea that is life—we so want them to be true. But because our childhood selves created them and because they are myths, they self-destruct under the slightest pressure. When that happens, instead of looking for reality-based beliefs to replace them, we scramble to re-assert our "shoulds" just as they were. They feel like old friends. They're anything but. They're nasty kids that pull the plug on the hot water in our tub of life.

If my "should" says I must be perfect, I could become obsessive about, say, preparing perfect meals for friends or family. That's a good thing on the surface, but it's not so good when I try to achieve impossible standards. And there will always come a time that I will show my imperfection, and beat myself up for it. Perfectionist strategies come from outer mind. They give us no peace or happiness. They just keep us on the run.

The List

When I put my "should" list together, I was shocked. I had been trying to get the whole world to move in lockstep with my fears. Others were supposed to change to suit me. Why didn't they? The answer was obvious when I thought about it. They were too busy trying to get *me* to change to suit *them*. Instead of understanding the basic flaw in my thinking—that I needed to make some shifts—I blamed them for their stubbornness. When I probed my deepest beliefs to discover the fears that were running me, these four stood out.

Shoulds	Fears	Reality
#1. *I should be perfect.* Whenever I saw my imperfection, I grew angry or embarrassed. I could not forgive myself for the slightest slip. *(Example: I spent six months in grad school in deep depression because I got a C+ on an important test.)*	I was afraid of uncertainty. Perfectionism allowed me to believe I was safe and superior in a changing world. I did not like people who were smarter than I was because that meant I was less than perfect. My child-sized "should" said I had to be at the top of the heap, or I was nothing.	We are all in the same boat in Earth School. Life's uncertainties are just opportunities for learning. Perfectionism is a sand castle waiting for a wave. Perfectionists take no joy in what is before them. They focus on the knothole, the spoiled spot, and the wrinkles.
#2. *No one should ever tell me what to do.*	If someone else could control my actions, I wasn't queen of my domain—a terrifying thought.	People like me who automatically resist others' ideas and suggestions miss the synergy possible with collaboration. We go our own hardheaded way, and we pay for it.
#3. *The world should dance to my tune.* Everything should be the way I want it to be.	If anything inconveniences me—including being put on hold or finding that the store is out of my brand of coffee—that proves I don't have the kind of grand cosmic control that outer mind says I should have.	Every inconvenience is an Earth School pop quiz.
#4. *Everyone I love should want to meet all of my expectations.*	If I am not the center of their universe, they are not under my control.	99.9999% of the people on this Earth are the centers of their own universes. That will not change anytime soon.

Devastating Discovery

My discovery of the "shoulds" that ran me for so many years was devastating at first. My very foundation was full of holes. "Ms. Perfect" definitely wasn't. I was "just folks" underneath it all. Eventually, though, that realization brought me a freedom I had never known. I didn't have to hide the truth from myself or anyone else. I no longer needed an acceptable persona to hide behind. And that's the point. Be glad when you find a "should." It's a nugget. Now, you can work with it. If you can't see it, it owns you.

When you discover a "should," realize that outer mind has used it against you since forever. Try not to blame yourself. If your "should" says you should not have to wait in long lines or put up with traffic jams or lost car keys (that you should never be inconvenienced)—you are not alone. Many people embrace that "should." They are all reacting to the fear beneath it—the fear that life is simply beyond their conscious control. Which it is.

If you can come to forgive yourself for negative or false beliefs that you have embraced for so many years, you can forgive others. Everyone around us has "shoulds." There's no shame in it. The only shame (as in "too bad," not "guilt") is if we recognize "shoulds" and do nothing about them.

> ### Reflection on Perfection
> *As an editor, I used to get very full of myself when I found a grammatical mistake or a typo in a manuscript. That continued until I realized how imperfect all of us are—including me. Do you ever struggle with a desire for perfection? Does the pursuit of perfection give you a sense of inner peace or does it chase you on to the next project—and the next? Is nothing ever good enough? Are you tired of running? Is there an alternative?*

Fear Triggers Anger

If fear is at the root of our "shoulds," why do we more commonly feel anger than fear when challenged? That's because people don't like feeling afraid and helpless. Anger makes us think we're in control, whether we are or not. If I choose to scream insults at someone just because I can get away with it, I am acting out of fear. My loud voice makes me think I'm powerful, but feel my racing heart. If I were coming from a place of real power, my heart would be at peace, and so would I. And, chances are, I would not be screaming.

I was driving on a road in rural Oregon recently, intent on finding an unfamiliar address. Suddenly, I heard a loud *HONK!* I was blocking a huge, chrome-plated SUV that belonged to a large, angry man. My immediate reaction was startled fear, but because I was paying attention to my emotions, I marveled as fear changed into anger at the speed of thought. I went from *"I'm so sorry I'm in your way"* to *"What do you mean, honking at me, jerk?"* No matter how it disguised itself, though, fear was still the root emotion.

I continued to feel upset even after I let the SUV pass. What was that about? I sat by the side of the road, trying to learn from life. If I went with the emotion-driven, outer mind thinking process, I'd keep on blaming the SUV driver and I would learn nothing. I wanted to find the "should" that had triggered my anger.

Suddenly, there it was: *"I should be perfect."* That driver had committed the unforgiveable crime of pointing out my mistake. Why did that bother me so much? First of all, that "should" is almost as old as I am. I created it when I was trying to feel safe in an unpredictable world. Bad things don't happen to perfect people, right? It makes complete sense—to a child. The reality was this: Life happens. To make this experience into a learning opportunity, I decided to keep a closer eye on how my driving affected others. My anger gone, I started up the car and continued the search for that unfamiliar address, but with greater awareness.

What happens if we don't engage with the fears that are moving behind our emotions? Nothing. We stay on the outer mind merry-go-round. We continue to get angry at what has always angered us. We stay in our self-destructive cycles. We judge and blame others. We keep on trying to get other people to change—and we do not learn or grow because we're squinting in the wrong direction.

All Fear or Love?

Every choice we make does come down to fear or love, but that doesn't always seem to make sense. When I do my taxes on time instead of getting an extension, it's not "love" I have in mind. It's more like a decision to do what needs doing instead of something that entertains me. Doing what's right and what needs doing is actually "love" if you think about it, but the use of the word "love" in this situation may feel like a stretch. If it's easier for you to say you are making a choice based on habit vs. conscious thinking or fear vs. courage or outer mind vs. soul mind instead of fear vs. love, use the language that works for you. The spirit of the words is what counts, not the words themselves.

Invisible Emotions

Most of us think of emotions as the major leaguers—jealousy, passion, revenge, hatred, and so on. We don't think much about the invisible emotional states, including stress, anxiety, frustration, and irritation. But we should. They are as important as the heavy hitters. Vengeance, for example, isn't something most of us dine on every day. Irritation is. Stress is. Frustration is. If we don't learn how to work with invisible emotions, that immature outer mind uses them to wield power over us. Invisible emotions take a major and unnecessary toll on the progress, happiness, and peace of most of the people on this planet.

Stress makes for emotional pain when it's the result of fighting against what *is*. Resentment, tension, and resistance can become a way of life. Unless we look for long-term stress's source, rather than focusing on relieving the symptom, the pot continues to boil. We stay fixated on the bubbles, but we don't reach around to turn off the fire. Ongoing stress can become a powerful guide. Sometimes, it points toward accepting reality with grace and gratitude. Sometimes, it points to the need for change.

Talia was on the production staff of a large, well-respected journal. She spent so many hours at the office every week that she kept a pillow and blanket stuffed under her desk. The journal was expanding at that time by 15% every year. Raised to embody a powerful work ethic, Talia's "should" said she had to accept each new task without question or complaint out of fear that others would see her as weak or maybe incompetent. She was neither, but her "should" was in charge. The reality was that the job was killing her. Talia's close friend suggested she hire people to cover the predictable expansion at the journal six months early. *"By the time they're needed,"* he said, *"they'll be up to speed."* She tried it. Eight months later, she took her pillow and blanket home. Talia's friend helped her see stress not as something she had to bear until the inevitable burnout, but as an early-warning signal that could be used to enlist soul mind's creativity.

Anxiety is another invisible emotion. Worry-warts see trouble around every corner. Anxiety makes us prepare flat-out for an upcoming test or speech or event, but we know that no matter how hard we work, it's not enough. It can't be. Author Gail Sheehy takes another perspective. She believes the solution to ongoing anxiety (or any other problem, for that matter) does not lie outside ourselves. It's closer to the bone. She says,

"When you have self-respect, you have enough." And maybe that's all there is to it. When we spend our lives looking outside ourselves for vindication or validation, no matter how much we get, it can never be enough. A little self-respect, though, goes a long way.

How about the low-level anger of frustration when we can't get tickets to a concert? How about irritation, another low-level anger, when someone changes our plans for us? *"What of it?"* we say. *"Isn't that normal?"* Yes, it is. That's because most people react normally to these invisible emotions on automatic. Maybe we're embarrassed that we waited until the last minute to order the concert tickets. We don't like that feeling so we stomp around in frustration, instead. Maybe we try to find someone else to blame. That's a growth opportunity lost. On the other hand, we may decide to make reservations earlier next time. That's a growth opportunity used.

How about changed plans? Let's say the boss cancelled your trip to Hawaii at the last minute. You may get irritated. Most people would. You may *stay* irritated, upset, and angry. You may allow this experience to sour your relationship with the boss. Even if you try not to show it, you sweat resentment. I know a woman who lost a job that she was born to do for that very reason.

What's on the surface—the cancelled vacation—is never what's important. It's how we use our irritation for the purpose of growth. Could this experience motivate you to stop hanging on to this job for the sake of so-called security and go find one that's a better fit? If so, you just struck gold. Having our plans changed can force us to spend time thinking deeply about the traps we've created for ourselves. What's your priority—your son's graduation or keeping the boss happy? Your mortgage or your life? Swallowed anger is never rich in nutrition.

On the other hand, maybe you actually were the one and only person with the expertise to do what the boss needed done. So just do it. And let the upset go. The beach isn't going anywhere.

If we're not used to paying attention to emotions, it helps to go slowly. This is a fertile field and worth the effort. You may want to start making yourself aware of emotions as they come up. Feel them—don't run away. Just feel them. Then, pull back a little and observe them. They are, after all, only a ripple across your mind, a ripple that you feel in your body. Emotions are both mental and physical, but they are not fixed forever in place. Your internal weather will change as surely as the weather outside always does.

Every emotion holds a key that can help us understand what moves us to do what we do, think what we think, feel what we feel, and say what we say. When we turn that key, we move either toward outer mind or soul mind. Blaming others is easy. That's an automatic outer mind reaction. Examining the chickens we brought home to roost, instead, is not so easy. If we can't blame someone else, no one's onstage but us. Even if we can't find that we did anything wrong, we can always learn something about ourselves in the process.

If we do not look inside, we can't see what's pulling our strings. If we are run by unidentified fears, every door looks locked. Every window becomes a wall.

Remember that no matter what happens, you still have you. Trust that you will find a way. Look to your soul mind. Expect doors to open. It's been said that love will find a way. There is a universal love that makes this and all worlds rotate. That's the love we seek. It can give us peace or it can bring us a totally unexpected Earth School situation— another opportunity. Great things happen when we no longer allow outer mind to have its way with us by using the well-worn emotion card.

Take every chance to discover more about this person you live with, this "you." I apologized to a beloved family member once for bottling something up and creating distance between us, instead of sharing how I really felt. She told me we should trust in our hearts and not get lost in our fears. Those words gave me the courage to explore difficult places with her without fearing I would lose her—or myself—along the way.

How can we work with the "shoulds" to get past fear and arrive at a truth when we are walking along, head in the clouds, and the ground drops away in front of us?

Beginning "Shoulds"

I was driving around downtown, looking for a parking space at a large, busy festival. A friend's son was slated to sing onstage in a few minutes. My intuition had actually warned me that parking would be tight, but I chose to ignore it.

I was getting upset, so I looked for my underlying "should." I found that I was afraid I would miss the performance and my friend would blame me. This fear was rooted in my perfectionist "should." If I didn't arrive on time, I'd be proving my imperfection. The moment I recognized that, I laughed at my less-than-perfect self. My stress disappeared.

Without that "should," my mind was freed from its tight focus on finding a parking spot where none existed. Now, it had the energy to come up with a creative solution. I realized that I could probably still make the performance if I drove far enough away. Parking three blocks from the festival, I walked quickly back to the stage, took a seat, waved and smiled encouragement to my friend's son, and enjoyed the show. I also enjoyed the knowledge that I had stepped outside of my "shoulds."

Intermediate "Shoulds"

Emotions grow more complicated in conflicts with other people. We may feel admiration, jealousy, anger, and love—all at the same time and all toward the same person. The other person can feel real affection toward us plus a desire to humiliate so he can feel superior. With so many emotions swirling about, how can we get a handle on them?

Let's look at a two-person conflict. It's just this other person and you—no one else. In any dynamic with another person, you can truly know only one side of it—your side. The other person's side is his or her responsibility. No matter how much we want to believe that we are being controlled, hurt, or destroyed by another person, the responsibility for how we respond is ours alone. And even if we believe that our happiness depends on another person's becoming more loving, less selfish, more outgoing, less focused on an old girlfriend or boyfriend, or more introspective, that is all make-believe. Our happiness does not depend on what other people do. It depends on our learning how to come from who we really are at the level of soul mind.

Perhaps a childhood friend and you are no longer able to pretend that love, as the two of you know it, conquers all. One of you has changed and grown, but the other has stayed pretty much the same. "Sherry" is feeling threatened by your widening perspective. Both of you have long known that this friendship could last only if you focused on the sisterly love between you, and not on your differences.

You may decide that you can no longer ignore those differences. You want the balance of power to shift toward greater equality. You have several choices—a courageous choice to face change together, a fearful choice to turn the relationship to stone, keeping it just as it is, or a choice to break up. Only the two of you will know whether that final choice is made out of fear or out of love.

Counseling may help, but not if one party is positive that all change has to be made by the other party. Every relationship is created by two people. Whatever it looks like on the outside, it meets the needs of both in the beginning. If those needs change, and the two are going to stay together, both parties must be willing to work toward empowering each other. On the other hand, maybe the relationship was doomed from the start. In that case, what's important becomes not blaming—not what the other person did or didn't do—but what you learned in Earth School and can take on to the next classroom.

Acting out of your integrity does not mean that the decision is easy. It can be very painful. The sense of loss may be profound. The emotional connection, the wish to keep this comfy old-shoe relationship, may rub hard against the awareness that it does not challenge you to grow, to become a better person than you already are. And if you want that challenge, you may find that this particular friendship has become one size too small.

If a relationship is unequal, if it is based on your being less than what you are so someone else can feel powerful by comparison, or vice versa, you will arrive at an impasse again and again. Any relationship that depends on keeping one person weak so that the other can feel strong will circle back to a choice between living on autopilot and living consciously, between peace at any price and being true to ourselves. The relationship can be between friends, husband and wife, parent and child, lovers, co-workers—any two people.

The pain that binds unequal relationships may feel almost comfortingly familiar. But if one person begins to grow, that shakes the relationship's foundation. The reaction can be swift: *"Change back!"*

In time, the subordinate person may weigh the fear of being alone and unloved vs. the courage to live in integrity, alone or not. The dominant person may choose to discover the joys and uncertainties of power-sharing. It's a simple but not easy choice between outer mind and soul mind.

It's not that one way is right and the other is wrong. People make choices for all kinds of reasons. But inner growth starts by recognizing why we make our choices, and then moving in the direction that we know in our hearts is forward.

A word of caution—it's much easier to see myths at work in the lives of other people than it is to dig into our own fears and beliefs. But unless you want to lose some close connections, don't share the "shoulds" and the fears you see in others' lives. They won't thank you for it. Use them, instead, as treasure maps that lead you to find more of your own "shoulds."

Advanced "Shoulds"

The hardest experiences bring our fears and beliefs into sharp relief. Answers are not easy. When a young woman I had mentored became my boss, I spent much of a day in pain. This situation did not fit my belief that no one should tell me what to do. I really liked my job and my new boss, so the problem was only with me.

Digging around in my simmering emotions, I recognized every one of them. Most were of the one-up, one-down variety. How could she become my boss when I was her senior? How could she decide what I should do when I had made those decisions for years without input from anyone? I was reading from a script I had often followed in the past. Once more, I had taken a troubling situation, made the mental worst of it, and allowed my outer mind to step front and center.

This was clearly an opportunity for a conscious choice. I wanted to be able to lay everything out before me, figure out the "shoulds," the fears, and the reality, but I could not. I was drowning.

Finally, I remembered what the lecturer had told us years back. *"When everything falls apart and you cannot find a solution, say, 'This I leave to my soul mind.'"* I knew that if soul mind is the architect of my life, this experience had purpose. If I reacted out of habit, I would lose the lesson.

I said the words of release over and over. As I repeated them, a sense of peace and comfort replaced my stubborn resistance to change. I was opening myself to fresh possibilities and energy, to a better, closer relationship with someone I care about and respect. This was clearly a new cycle that held nothing but promise, no matter what outer mind told me. I embraced it and looked back only once—to clearly identify outer mind's fingerprints all over this experience. I memorized the shape of those fingerprints in preparation for the pop quiz that surely lies somewhere out there in my future.

Courage

When we're working to track down our "shoulds," we never get anywhere without crossing one of those swinging rope bridges—the kind that hang spectacularly suspended far above torrential rivers in South

America. I don't know about you, but the fear I have around crossing a rope bridge ranks right up there with getting nibbled on by sharks. A major lesson in Earth School is courage, but not movie courage. This courage calls on us to face down our fears and weaknesses, one by one. It asks us to communicate from our depths without blaming anyone else and by being willing to admit our errors. For many of us, that's a whole new language.

Internal Dialogues

It was years before I could talk about interpersonal problems with someone close to me. Instead, I would have dialogues with myself. A forgotten birthday? An inappropriate choice of restaurants? It never occurred to me that a friend had simply lost track of the day or that my boyfriend thinks diners are suitable places to celebrate special occasions. Instead, I filled my head with rants: *"She (or he) doesn't love me anymore. It's over."* Maybe the boyfriend was short on cash that week. I couldn't know without asking. And I couldn't ask.

Internal dialogues come from outer mind, from fear. Sharing what's going on with us and asking for a reality check from the other person is the only way to get to soul mind from the quicksand that is the hallmark of outer mind.

Make More Mistakes

We all make mistakes. It's okay. We should make more of them. That's how we learn, how we build a skill. It's how we build a life worth living. Everything we overcome frees our hearts from fear, one strand at a time.

Exercise: Buy or designate a spiral notebook as your spiritual journal. A short list of possible "shoulds" follows. For practice, look for the fears that may lie behind these six "shoulds." Then, try to figure out what the truth or reality could be behind those fears. Whether or not you claim these "shoulds" as your own, work with them for practice in understanding what others believe.

- I should get what I want without having to work hard for it.
- If I am sensitive to other people's feelings, they should be sensitive to mine.
- I should never have to wait for what I want.

- The people I love should know I love them without my having to say the words.
- Other people should not treat me with disrespect.
- My friends should always be there for me when I need them.

Now, list as many of your own "shoulds" as you can. Include the fears that energize them, and the truths you discover. From today's perspective, you may discover that some of your childhood-based "shoulds" are amusing. That's good. Laughing at ourselves shakes up old ideas, aerates the lungs, and enables us to suck in great quantities of clean, fresh reality.

Emotions and Feelings

In the English language, we use the words "emotions" and "feelings" interchangeably. When I say *"I love you,"* am I expressing an emotion or a feeling? How about *"I hate you"*—emotion or feeling? To help us figure out the differences between these sometimes frightening, uplifting, shocking, or transcendent parts of ourselves, the lecturer created an artificial division. He called what's connected to the outer mind "emotions." He put "feelings" into soul mind's basket. Confused? You won't be for long.

Outer Mind and Emotions

Imagine that you are the outer mind of the person who is reading these words. You have grown powerful. Your voice is loud in the reader's ears while you work to keep control of the steering wheel of life. You may distract the reader with the fire and ice of emotions—the agonies of unrequited love, the competitive rat race of a career, a self-destructive battle with food or alcohol or drugs or any of the other heartbreaking or fear-induced activities common to this planet. The goal of this kind of outer mind-directed, Earth-bound emotionality is to keep the reader's focus anywhere *except* on the steering wheel.

The outer mind uses hatred, jealousy, greed, and selfishness to bind us to our soap operas. Outer mind's fear-based beliefs may convince us that we can never have enough, be enough, or do enough. It tells us that the people we spend our lives caring for are ungrateful and unloving.

Soul mind, though, breathes into us through feelings of gratitude, kindness, compassion, honesty, integrity, humility, and love.

What about that word, "love"? People have done terrible things in its name. A jealous husband may raise his gun, saying, *"If I can't have you, nobody can!"* Isn't this love? *Passionate* love? No. It's possession. Basically, it's a control issue. We can't own another person. No matter how great our inner turmoil, it does not give us the right to dictate how others should feel, or how long they should live.

Lust is powerful, but it is not love. People who abuse others mentally, emotionally, or physically may call what they do "love," but consider this: Love is honest. It has no devious motives. Love does not beat others down to feed an ego. When we love, we want what's best for the other person as part of a caring and delicate balance of their needs and ours. Love is created on a level playing field—those who express love as a *feeling* are equals. Love does not ask us to give up who we are so we can be loved by another. Love is playful, warm, forgiving, and forbearing.

The lecturer stated more than once that real love is not given one moment, and taken away the next. Love that is love remains. It may get battered by circumstances and tested to the extreme, but real love has nowhere to go. It just *is*. You may decide to part from someone you love for excellent reasons, but a place in your heart continues to vibrate to that person's name. If it doesn't, it was not love you knew, but something else.

Soul Mind and Feelings

If there is a foundational feeling, one from which all other feelings arise, it is the universal consciousness of love, of oneness—sometimes called God. And we all have that consciousness within.

Humility, the readiness to serve others when needed, is sourced in this love. With humility, our better angel gives to the better angel of another. We may not be able to see that angel very clearly in the other person, but we know—through love—that it's in there somewhere.

Honesty, the contentment that comes from enjoying what we have earned, with no desire for what belongs to someone else, is a feeling. Honesty is closely related to integrity, to living in the world so that the best of who we are inside is expressed outside. Honesty and integrity are love-based, as is compassion, the feeling that understands the suffering of others and wants to help without expecting payback.

Patience, perseverance, and adaptability are all feelings. If they don't sound quite like "feelings" to you, picture the emotional turmoil their opposites create—the impatience, the nervous desire to grab at the *new* new thing, the determination to have things go our way, no matter what.

Emotions and Feelings Reflect Outer Mind and Soul Mind

Emotions and feelings exist along a continuum, just like outer mind and soul mind do. To get a sense of the difference between them, close your eyes (if you're in an appropriate place) and feel the difference in your energy when you imagine, for example, aggressiveness. See the anger, feel the barely held-back rage of someone who is out of control, the desire to tell someone else what to do, or else!

Now, imagine assertiveness. Picture someone who stands up for herself in a respectful way. She chooses quiet courage and maintains her principles when challenged. Really feel the differences between these two words—"aggressiveness" and "assertiveness." That's the difference between emotion and feeling.

Now, try impatience and patience. Say, for example, you're in the grocery store checkout line with a shopping cart full of food. You have guests arriving for dinner at 7 p.m. It's now 6. And you're a 20-minute drive away from home. A woman ahead of you can't find her credit card. She's dumping everything out of her purse onto the checkout counter while you watch, frustrated. Feel your impatience.

Now, try imagining the same situation, but this time, you choose to use it for patience practice. You take some deep breaths. You know you won't make it home to get everything done by the time your guests arrive. Will this be the first time in their lives that they have ever had to wait? Will the world end because you are late? Can you use the time to do a stand-up, eyes-open meditation? Can you send the increasingly upset woman (who still can't find her credit card) a warm thought or two? Can you smile at someone else in line? Chat for a few minutes? Feel the feeling of patience. Now, feel again the emotion of impatience. Feel the difference.

The emotions at one end of the continuum are not "bad" any more than the outer mind is bad. Emotions have a couple of important purposes. Not only can they help us figure out what's going on when we're in overwhelm, but they also point us toward their corresponding feelings at the other end of the continuum. For example, selfishness points us in the direction of selflessness. Think of the evolution of the self-centered baby into the child who learns to share a toy or a favorite food. It's a slow process.

We start to overcome selfishness when we are touched by love for another or when we see how destructive selfishness is—and we decide to grow beyond it toward the selflessness at the other end of the continuum. We are not selfish one day and selfless the next. Most of us move along that continuum at a fairly leisurely rate. I know I do.

Evolution of Emotions into Feelings: Love

As attitudes and beliefs evolve, emotions transition into feelings. I used to think of love as something that made the palms of my hands tingle. It killed my appetite and made me sleepless and obsessive. At school or at work, my mind was filled with thoughts of *him*—how he looked, what he said, what he might say, and when we could next be together. Love demanded that he put me at the center of his life, just as he was at the center of mine. I would sit at home, waiting for his call. I accepted no invitations if they might conflict with his plans. If he allowed anything or anyone to compete with me for his time or affections, he didn't really love me. It was all or nothing. That's love as an *emotion.*

Love as a *feeling* began after I understood that I was an important part of his life, but I wasn't all of it. I started to appreciate his other friends, rather than being jealous of them. I accepted that he had interests that did not include me.

Love really started moving from an emotion into a feeling when I became glad that he had these other friends and interests. They expanded and enriched his life. They made him happier. And his happiness, not just mine, had become important. Instead of the jealousy, fear, and obsession that had colored love as an emotion, my feelings had grown and developed into trust and the willingness to let him be who he is. That took time and conscious effort—and the awareness that if I didn't grow, I would lose the opportunity to love and be loved by this particular man in a way that I, as a perennial emotional adolescent, had never known.

The more we go on automatic, the less likely it is that we will find new and creative ways of dealing with difficult situations. If, for example, we always storm out of the house during a disagreement, we lose the opportunity to learn. We may typically slam the door on the way out. Maybe next time, we leave—but we close the door softly. Or maybe we don't leave at all. Maybe we count to ten. Maybe we breathe or meditate.

Anger burns so brightly that it may blot out what's behind it, but that's where the real issue is. Is our anger hiding the self-righteousness of the "perfect" person? Do we use anger to make sure we win at all costs? Are we trying to manipulate others? Do we automatically go into a rage because that's what we saw growing up? When we least want to connect with someone else, the heart of the lesson may lie in our willingness to move toward connection. We may want to consider asking questions and sharing what we feel, rather than burning bridges.

Emotions are valuable—especially the prickly ones. And as little as we may want to admit it, it's unlikely that we are 100% right while the other person is 100% wrong. We benefit from any experience if it gives us a deeper understanding of our shadows.

Evolution of Emotions into Feelings: Grief

"Snap out of it. Time to move on!" We've all heard the world's business-model advice to the broken hearted. Friends and relatives who are uncomfortable around our grief try to cheer us up, distract us, or convince us that we'll "get over it." If we've lost a love, they remind us about all those other fish who are eagerly swimming in the sea. We, however, are neither cheered nor ready to go fishing.

In this culture, we are not raised to use grief for growth. It's treated more like a low-level, self-indulgent illness—the right words or a little vacation are supposed to bring us back to the smiling person we were, just as if nothing had ever happened. A woman I know lost her daughter to cancer. *"Kelly was a generous, caring human being,"* she says. *"But my friends and family are tired of hearing me talk about her. They don't know what to say to help me. I don't need words of sympathy. I just want them to remember her life with me and take joy in who she was."*

Many people don't understand the value of the grieving process. They want us to ignore it, largely out of their own fears about the future—the deaths and losses we all face if we live long enough. Grief, though, is not just some bad habit that needs to be hidden from others' eyes. It hears only the griever's drummer. And for good reason.

Everything in life is crucial to our growth. That includes grief. If we try to blot out the pain with externals—with parties, shopping, food, or anything else that allows us to pretend that great and important things are not at work in our depths—the opportunity that grief represents is lost. That deep pain asks us to be quiet, to slow down for awhile, to go within and maybe spend time out in Nature.

Grief is a natural process with its own heart-based rhythm. It moves us into a slower gear. That's because while we grieve, everything we experience flows first through the heart and then through the mind.

Minds are not accustomed to a second-banana connection to the heart. They don't quite know what to do. We may find ourselves forgetful while we grieve. We lose our keys. Misplace our shoes. We skip dinner—and remember it hours later. Our thoughts veer off into memories. We're "not ourselves." If we try to act normal while we don't feel normal, life loses its flow. Fighting with grief is as effective as boxing with the wind.

We would like to believe that time heals all things. It doesn't—not if we think time will do the job for us. All by itself, time does not heal anything. We heal ourselves by examining and using what's going on inside productively. Or we miss the opportunity.

When we break a leg, it heals faster if we get out of bed and hobble about on crutches. That's because the body was designed to move, just like emotions and feelings. Stagnation of any kind is unhealthy. We reach carefully, gently within to understand where grief wants to take us, and what it can help us learn.

Recently, I lost someone. I spun into grief mode on autopilot. My angry outer mind threw rocks at "the enemy." After a few hours of going over and over the same territory, I told myself that if everything happens for a reason, this experience could not be the one and only exception to that rule since time began. And so I sat with it. And felt it. As my heart and my mind communicated, I understood another deep "should" of mine—that no one should hurt my friends. But the reality was that what was done was done. The situation was out of my control. I felt stymied. How could I respond in a way that was respectful to the spirit of our friendship?

Eventually, I wrote down some qualities I will miss most about this particular friend—his loyalty, his cracked sense of humor, and his courage. And finally, this thought came to mind: *"Maybe I can learn to be more loyal, laugh more about wonderfully crazy things, and be willing to stand up faster for what I believe is right."* That thought could not bring him back. But it did soften the hurt. It allowed me to tap into love, instead. And that's when the anger began to subside. It was only then, when I reached a new perspective on my grief, that I understood the purpose of the anger. It was an arrow I could use on a path toward growth.

The experience of grief and grief's timetable are different for each person. Our inner self can tell us when it's time to move on—if we listen. It's all right to spend time in the land of grief, but it's a mistake to be buying a mortgage there. Our hearts grow brittle if we stuff them with nothing but memories. Staying stuck in grief keeps it limited to an emotion. Grief offers us a unique opportunity. If we allow grief to evolve from an emotion into a feeling, it scours us out and leaves a space behind. In that space, we may find the seeds of compassion growing.

In the end, if all we do is drown in the emotion of grief or sorrow, we choose drama over love, loss over gain, and death over life—not what the people we love, and have lost, would want for us.

Emotion or Feeling?

If we still wonder whether something is an emotion or a feeling, it helps to weigh whether fear or love is at work. Do we feel superior or inferior to someone? That's emotion. Emotions always place people in the "one-up, one-down" position. If we feel desperate to have someone love us, for example, that's emotion. We have made that person powerful, made ourselves powerless, and called it love.

The regular practice of rooting around in our own fears and motivations can help us distinguish between love as an emotion and love as a feeling. Why do we want what we want? Why do we *really* want it? Are we perhaps looking for a trophy lover? Or some other kind of trophy? Outer mind loves trophies.

In a nutshell, feelings uplift the heart. Emotions that run us shrink both heart and life. Feelings move us toward one another, while emotions separate us. Emotions are what come up when we know the cupboard has only one can of soup—and we hide it.

Emotions can make the dance floor slippery. We all have setbacks—we take three steps forward and one or two back. No setback should convince us that all is forever lost. That's outer mind's voice in our ears. Setbacks are just opportunities to try again.

In Earth School, we cannot control what others do. We cannot even control what happens to us. What we can control is how we walk in the world, and why.

Chapter Six
Earth School: Movable Classroom

*L*essons lie in what we notice and in what we overlook. Life asks us to seek our source, and live in harmony with soul mind, each other, and ourselves. That's pretty much it. And that's a lot. We may be convinced that happiness is found only outside the envelope of our own skin—in the perfect mate or job. Real happiness lies in mastering whatever scoops us up and spits us out.

Everything that comes about is the result of something else that happened previously. We cannot cheat, bargain, or buy our way out of our lessons, the lecturer told us. Nor can we weep them away.

Can we retrogress? Can we lose what we have learned? No. Something that has been fully learned is ours. If we trip over a lesson we thought we had mastered—perhaps the tendency to overreact to what others say or do—it only means a piece of the lesson still needs work.

We are here to learn from our experiences, our mistakes, and the mistakes of others, he said. Most people do that the hard way, by trial and error. We stumble, fall, and pick ourselves up. When I was nine, I stole a packet of pencils from a store. My mother made me go right back and return it. As I handed my loot over to a saleswoman, I felt a full-body blush come on. I still remember running all the way home, trying to outpace the shame. My personal curriculum is packed with things still not overcome, but that was my graduation day from Shoplifting 101.

With conscious practice, we can learn not by trial-and-error, but through the process of realization. Realization is when we get ourselves to leave home a few minutes early for an appointment—we who are famously late for everything. It's when we decide that inhaling a box of Dove® ice cream bars will do us more harm than good, and we put the package back in the grocery store freezer. As you might imagine, realization is easier and faster than trial-and-error. It's also a couple of notches up on the evolutionary ladder. True teacher that it is, soul mind just wants us to learn. If it takes a thwack across the shoulders to get our attention, thwacked we will be. Trial-and-error? Or realization? Our choice.

We make choices all day long as we move through space-time. *Pay bills tonight or watch TV? Run that red light, or risk being late? Pretend I didn't see her or spend 30 minutes hearing more grandkid stories?* Everything we do, think, feel, or say calls for a choice—and those choices become a part of our energy field. Each choice affects the frequency of our overall energy, lifting or lowering it. If we start to sensitize ourselves to these fluctuations, we can feel the internal shifts.

Choices react on our energy field much like piano notes react on our hearts, minds, and bodies. In Western music theory, some note combinations are harmonious, while others create tension. Harmonious notes relax and please us and tension-producing notes feel "off" until they are resolved into a harmonious chord. Our choices affect us in much the same way.

Although the music fades, our choices stay with us. Like all molecules of energy, choices never completely disappear—neither the harmonious nor the inharmonious ones. Choices move us forward or they keep us in "park" until the next opportunity. If we then react as we habitually do—with the same anger or resentment or fear or arrogance—we stay in park, which leads to pain. How else can soul mind get our attention?

We are in school 24/7 x 365. When we stub a toe, it's not just a toe stub. It's an Earth School pop quiz. When we cut ahead in line, we're not just thumbing our noses at everyone behind us. It's a test—for us and for everyone who's watching. Some in line won't care. Some will choke on indignation. One may say, *"I was here first!"* Then, what? The possibilities are endless. Every whim, hunger, inconvenience, surprise, disaster, demand, need—anything—calls for a choice. And every choice makes a difference.

We can't always know the outcome of our choices, although it's helpful to consider alternatives before we climb onto a roof slippery with rain in our bare feet. Even more important than the choices themselves, however, is knowing the motivation behind them. When I was unemployed years back, a headhunter suggested I submit my resume to a well-known company. To satisfy stockholders, the company was planning drastic cuts in employee benefits. Human resources needed a spin doctor—someone who could convince employees that the cutbacks were actually a *plus*. The headhunter thought I would be ideal for the job—after all, hadn't I made my living on television? We all know what *that* means.

I was powerfully tempted, partly because I so identified my worth with what I did for a living. My outer mind said, *"Take the job. If you don't, someone else will!"* A high-energy hum was singing inside me. I was hungry for a good salary, the prestige, and even, yes, the challenge of figuring out how to twist the truth inside out and make it shine. This happened years before I re-opened that old box, but somehow I knew I was at a turning point and I made a choice. How could I stand to brush my teeth every morning while looking into the eyes of a woman who would do anything for money?

Chapter Seven
Earth School: Extended Human Family

*M*ost of our lessons, the lecturer said, center on other people. Our classmates sold us our insurance, cleaned our house, cut our hair, remodeled the kitchen, hired us, fired us, fixed our flat tire by the roadside, or explained the intricacies of quantum mechanics. It's the people we live with or love. Or hate. It's the teenager who cranks up her stereo with no respect for others' taste in music. It's everyone who comes our way.

If our aim is to align our own outer and soul minds, what do other people have to do with it? Why do we have to deal with their problems and karma, anyway? Why can't we just work on our own stuff? We could. It's possible to find an empty cave, let our hair grow, and munch on berries and twigs. But if we abandon the world, we miss the gifts our classmates offer us.

We learn much about the rugged hill country of the heart with members of this extended human family. Others help teach us what we cannot or will not learn on our own. We see weaknesses in others that we ignore in ourselves. Those weaknesses drive us crazy—until we figure out their source. Maybe you dislike people who squeeze every nickel. Could you be a bit of a cheapskate, too? Or maybe we can't stand friends who spend their money like water and then expect us to pay for dinner. It's the same lesson—just opposite ends of a continuum. Between the two extremes—the fear of not having enough vs. the unwillingness to take responsibility for ourselves—lies a wide range of possible unconscious and conscious choices.

I decided to test these ideas by taking a closer look at two broken friendships—one with a man and one with a woman. When I pictured Jeff and Evelyn, I felt self-righteous—they were wrong and I was right! That by itself was a powerful clue: My emotions were putting up a smokescreen and outer mind was at work. I didn't want to spend even one more minute thinking about either of those people. So I sat myself down and stared at my resentment and my sense of superiority toward them.

Jeff was arrogant, well-spoken, self-centered, domineering, angry, and profoundly opinionated. He would ramp up his powerful voice until it drowned out everyone else in the room. Believing my dislike of his approach showed how evolved I was, I was glad to see the friendship end when our differing temperaments led to a head-on collision over a small disagreement. So why was I still angry? That's when I saw my jealousy. Jeff had the nerve to act ugly (by my lights) and call it beautiful. He was willing to intimidate others into accepting his viewpoint while I was still mostly afraid of being anything but *nice*. Once I recognized that truth, outer mind's self-satisfied reasoning could no longer blind me. I wasn't going to start imitating Jeff, but I was tired of sitting on the sidelines of life, as nice people often do.

My "should" with Jeff was that civilized people were as quiet and polite as I was. My fear was that if I raised my voice, people would discover that I had thoughts that were different from theirs, and they would reject me. I would be alone. The reality was that my fear kept me living almost completely without principles, without those things that distinguish a human being from a door knob. With so few principles, I rarely needed any courage.

I decided to watch how I reacted to situations to see where my principles actually lived. I looked for what touched my heart and mind, what I wanted to contribute to, and what I wanted to be a part of. The exercise led to some positive changes that continue to this day.

The other broken friendship was quite different. Evelyn was an attractive UPS driver, currently unemployed. She picked an abusive partner and then filled friends' ears with stories about how awful the relationship was. Having been through similar experiences myself, I thought I could save her some time on that hard road. I would share my sad stories and what I'd learned from them. She repeatedly told me how much my words meant to her, but months passed and her life never changed.

The friendship lasted for almost a year. In the early months, I'd get angry and protective when she shared her boyfriend's latest insults. I'd say, *"How could he talk to you like that?"* or *"He should treat you with more respect!"* But during the last month before she left, I stopped making comments. I just listened. I felt I was being used, but I wasn't sure exactly how. As it turned out, we were using each other.

I felt relieved and also numb when I knew she wasn't coming back. Because numbness is not a natural emotion, I knew something was going on. What I found beneath the surface was anger—sour anger. As the star of her own soap opera, Evelyn had felt powerful. She had me as her goggle-eyed audience. My attention and sympathy were her applause. When I began to withdraw that energy, she went looking for a new audience.

All the dramaholic signposts were there—if I'd been willing to see them. As a recovering dramaholic myself, I knew better. But I didn't *do* better. I was getting emotional payback from wanting to rescue her. She was getting emotional payback by avoiding rescue. Without her soap opera, she had nothing.

Neither of us was growing through the friendship. I got upset with myself for giving my outer mind free rein—again. For letting myself be manipulated. Again. Next time, I told myself, I would recognize this co-dependent pattern sooner.

Emotions need to be looked at whenever we have problems with other people. I'm not talking feelings here. I'm talking down-and-dirty *emotions*. If we use just our heads to understand what's going on in Earth School, we'll miss the lesson every time. When we feel self-righteous toward someone, wounded beyond compare, we need to ask what that's all about. When our emotions make others the enemy (as in "us vs. them"), we haven't gone far enough. Anger starts to lose its sting only after we recognize ourselves somewhere inside the people who give us so much trouble.

Out among our classmates, we can't escape ourselves—as much as we might like to. Some people are so determined to live their own lives that they refuse to change just to please us. Imagine that! We may even wind up changing ourselves as a result of what we learn from them. I've done that—and been glad of it later, although I didn't like learning those dance steps at the time.

Still other people in this world inspire us. They may significantly pull us beyond where we are. Maybe that's why so many of us become "workshop junkies." It's disappointing to discover that while others can point the way, they can't walk our walk for us. Maybe our true journey begins when we stop looking for gurus and start living like one.

So, which do we choose? A solitary life, or one filled with others' messy humanity? We could decide to listen only to piano music written for the left hand. That music is beautiful. But it's limited—there's very little of it to be had. Just think what we would miss—the huge repertoire of piano music written for both hands! The beauty. The passion. The precision. The peace. The moments that burst our hearts open and enliven our souls.

Look around you. We are here among people. We may go somewhere else. For today, though, this is where we are. We learn by doing our best with what's at hand. A kind word or a smile for no particular reason—such things are never wasted.

The pain we experience among other human beings may be the most searing we will ever know. Grief is not the only kind of pain that can teach compassion. Once compassion is ours, it's ours forever. We will never again look at other people—or even at ourselves—in quite the same chilly way.

Reflections on the Underside

Many of the following have been, and sometimes still are, my stumbling blocks. Yours may be different, but you'll probably find one or two that remind you of you. And if not, maybe you'd like to try to name your own "dragons"—and consider what it would take to start taming them.

- *Taking what isn't ours just because we can*
- *Manipulating others to get what we want*
- *Believing that nothing we do is ever good enough*
- *Resenting having to do what we don't want to do*
- *Giving up on projects or people too easily*
- *Disliking authority figures just because they are authority figures*
- *Using accomplishments or abilities to make ourselves feel superior to others*
- *Withdrawing into silence to punish others*
- *Pushing to get our way no matter what*
- *Blaming*
- *Postponing what needs doing*
- *Staying stuck in our ways or ideas*
- *Being jealous of others' successes*
- *Being sure we're right*
- *Feeling we're victims of other people or our circumstances*
- *Always looking for a way to turn situations to our advantage*
- *Believing that changing other people will make us happy*

Chapter Eight
Earth School: Living Consciously

*B*abies start out knowing how to live consciously, but they lose the knack along the way. Look at how the very young interact with the world. Everything is *new*. A flower. The feel of cat fur. A smile or a frown. The young focus intently on each experience. They must learn to interpret what's going on, and react in a way that brings them what they want and avoids what they don't want. The young process and file experiences into their personal data banks. An entry can be as simple as *"parsnips—yuck."* Later, we take shortcuts. We don't have to taste a parsnip. The smell alone reminds us: Yuck pile. As we grow older, we don't have to smell a parsnip: *"Looks like a parsnip. Yuck."* Habitual ways of dealing with experience *("I've made up my mind, and that's that")* replace our earlier open-hearted, open-minded approach.

Have you ever driven from home to work, your mind busy with daydreams, your ears full of radio blat, and realized that you remember nothing between starting up the car and pulling into your parking spot? I have. Who was driving? As long as traffic is smoothly moving along, driving is handled by only a small portion of outer mind. The larger portion is concerned with angry rehashings of conversations past, scripting of future conversations, and mental meanderings—and it's always ready to take offense at the first driver who gets in our way. It's occupied with its toys—until danger brings it home. It's a split-second process between unconscious driving and conscious driving, and anything can happen in a split second.

Now, picture all the other drivers around us in the same sleepwalking state. How many accidents and near misses result from unconscious driving? To drive consciously for the entire trip, we would have to be aware of where we are and what's going on around us every moment. *"Why do that?"* you may ask. *"I like disconnecting. It keeps me from being bored."* In "Groundhog Day," a great old Bill Murray movie, Bill's character has to relive the same day repeatedly, making unconscious choice after unconscious choice until he learns the difference between lust and love, and until he becomes conscious enough to create a life that feels worth living.

I did not consciously choose distant or abusive men, but if one lived within 50 miles, our radar brought us together. I would have wept with fury if anyone had been so unfeeling as to say I had *chosen* them. Lovers happen to us. We all know that! At some point, though, we wonder how we can high-grade our dance partners. It doesn't work just to decide we will no longer be attracted to people who cheat on us or to force ourselves to manufacture a spark with someone who doesn't turn us on. I've tried that.

In my experience, we slowly begin to attract different kinds of people after we slowly begin to become different kinds of people. What we choose on an unconscious level shows where we are. Was a past lover vain, selfish, and inconsiderate? Is the new one ready to laugh at himself, ready to share—but still inconsiderate, still snapping his impatient fingers at waiters, still shouting incoherently at people who misplace his dry cleaning? He's so much better than the last one that we wonder if we can't just live with it. We don't want to lose this 66% fabulous man. We may try to convince ourselves that we are asking too much. We should be happy to be happy two days out of three, yes?

If we don't make conscious choices many times a day, we stay in default mode. We continue to ride the ruts dug deeply by family history, habit, bad relationships, fear and hopelessness, despair and pain. We don't consciously want to repeat our family history—not the bad part, anyway. Unless we make an effort to grow beyond it, though, it's almost impossible not to. *"I had a terrible childhood,"* we say. Some of us spend much of a lifetime still clinging to the long-dead past.

Our childhood does not determine what we become. We do. Childhood is only a launching pad. We try to understand what didn't work for us. We try to improve on what our parents did. If our parents did well, we build on what they taught us. If their parenting was a mix of good and bad, which it usually is, it's learning how to pick the best and leave the rest. It takes time to re-learn conscious living, and to expand on it so we go beyond the narrow focus of the self-centered younger version of ourselves. Where to start? Perhaps at the beginning. Did family members blame everyone but themselves? Did they hate or fear certain groups? Did they believe money determined worth? Did they raise us to believe we were little princes or princesses? Or that we were worthless? Wherever we started, I'm grateful to say, we don't have to stay there.

We may give up the dream of a college education, for example, because of family obligations. How do we feel about that? Do we release the dream in the knowledge that we are doing the right thing? Or do we burn with resentment? Earth School doesn't always give us what we want. It does give us what we need. Winning and losing—so important in our world—aren't even in the curriculum. We can choose to stay on the same unconscious treadmill for as long as we like. It feels like we're moving forward. We *are* moving. But not forward. So, what is "forward," as compared to standing still?

As babies, we were satisfied with full stomachs, affection, and reasonably clean diapers. Maybe we were stars and the world revolved around us. The next step was when someone else's needs and desires became as important to us as our own. After that, maybe we learned to care deeply about a circle of friends and family, and then our community. And if we reached the point where everyone on this planet felt like family, we had transformed ourselves. Not many of us get that far in a lifetime. We are probably not Gandhi, Mother Teresa, Martin Luther King, Jr., Helen Keller, Albert Einstein, Eleanor Roosevelt, or the Dalai Lama. But even with lesser goals than theirs, we can make good use of our time here. Each step beyond where we are right now moves us closer to who we really are.

Conscious choices come from soul mind. Ask yourself, *"Which choice calls for courage?"* Albert Einstein said insanity is doing the same thing over and over again and expecting different results. You and I are not insane, but we can be stubborn. If we choose to do what we've always done, we'll get what we've always gotten. Courage isn't found in ruts. To live fully, we need to come *from* something, be *for* something, not just *against* something.

We've all known fear. We've all had doubts or uncertainties. For some, though, fears and doubts don't come and go. They stay. Fear of dying, fear of becoming helpless, fear of losing a job, our looks, our health, or the one person we think makes life worth living—the list is long. Fear can take the joy out of anything. Fear of loss that shows up as jealousy can kill the love it's meant to protect. People who fear failure may never try to succeed.

A doubting mind can weigh on us as heavily as fear. It whispers, *"He brought me flowers only because he's covering something up."* It says, *"I don't trust anyone."* Doubt is always on the defensive. *"Why shouldn't I cheat? Everyone else does."* Doubts and fears live in the same dark outer mind neighborhood.

A tricky part of living in the now is learning how to be connected *and* free. Imagine reaching a point where it's not either/or—where it all comes together. Where we feel deeply—*and* we can allow the world and its people to spin freely as they will. Where we align ourselves with soul mind by living consciously, by growing poised in peace and courageous in principle, and by transcending fear and doubt. Wouldn't that be worth some effort?

> ### *Reflection on Security*
> *Seeking security, I once connected with the wrong man. I had convinced myself I was desperately in love. I was desperate, all right. But not in love. Think back. Have you ever made a life choice based on fear? What was the outcome? What do you know now that you did not know then?*

Choosing Wisdom

Few moments are more exhilarating than when we first allow ourselves to throw a light on a difficult experience and choose wisdom.

A friend owned a construction company in California. Carpenters, electricians, tile men, and others worked his projects. Most of them were older than Matthew. They were loud, tough, crude—and proud of it. Matthew was quality driven and soft-spoken. Some of the men liked to cut corners. Matthew would spot shoddy work—and politely request a re-do. They often ignored him. Skilled workers were hard to find in those boom times. Getting rid of every man with a bad attitude was not an option. Dominant-male behavior was what these men understood, respected, and obeyed, so Matthew learned to go into his "veins-popping" mode. Standing six inches from a man's face, Matthew would scream at him until he backed down. *"After I left the scene,"* said Matthew, *"I was Mr. Mellow again. I wasn't angry. It was all a game."* He had learned to use an emotion, instead of being at its mercy.

At the other end of that spectrum, I remember an incident in my late teens when I was working for a shipping company in Los Angeles. My fiery temper had no "off" button. My supervisor told me I'd be staying late at the office that night because she was leaving early for a long weekend in Palm Springs. It wasn't a request. It was an order. She triggered my "should" that said no one was supposed to tell me what to do. My anger meter instantly went from zero to 100. I saw red—literally. I looked out across an office filled with desks and 40 employees through a haze of my own blood. I had burst a blood vessel in my eye. Instead of using anger as a tool, anger used me. I was completely at its mercy—and at the mercy of outer mind.

Enlightenment is a funny word. To some, it's so far beyond the reach of ordinary mortals as to be like the sun—you can reach for it as hard and as long as you like, but you'll never more than warm your fingertips. I have seen that mastery of the inner fitness principles in the workbook that follows can guide a person toward another kind of enlightenment, an everyday enlightenment—one in which we eventually take a quantum leap into understanding what life is about, what we are about, and where we fit into a much larger and more joyous picture than the one we currently see.

Consider these thoughts: Enlightenment may not be just for the few, something that requires a spiritual athlete to pass a Herculean, once-in-a-lifetime test on the way to slipping through the eye of the needle. What if enlightenment comes about by the daily practice of simple, humble concepts, none of which carries much clout in what we call modern life? What if, indeed?

Chapter Nine
Workbook Introduction

*F*rom this point forward, you will be asked to weigh habits, connect with your deeper self on a daily basis, and consider different ways of looking at yourself and at your life.

Remember what you went through to learn how to ride a bicycle? You had to be patient enough to master the art of balancing on two wheels and steering at the same time. Only then could you fly. The same is true of building inner fitness. I ask you to partner with me in this process and trust that if you do it in more or less real time, day after day, you will gain far more than you would by racing through the stories, asking, *"What's next?"* Isn't this book about, perhaps, trying something different?

Each story is a single day's focus within the framework of the 28-day program. Rather than getting caught up in the content of the stories, try to look for the essence, the heart, the lessons in each story. And if you want to repeat a previous day's lesson and set of exercises, that's okay, too. The effect is cumulative—as you move through the lessons, you build on what you learned earlier. Don't worry about treating every experience that comes your way in life consciously. You couldn't. You would spend your days second-guessing yourself. Simply incorporate what you can as often as possible.

Life happens. Sometimes, you may have to skip a day. Even two. Don't obsess about doing this work for *exactly* 28 consecutive days. Don't let a passion for perfection tell you that you blew it, that all is lost. And don't rush it, trying to make up for lost time by doing two days' work in one. If you keep your eye on where you are going and pick up where you left off, you'll get there. And if you want to repeat the entire program at the end of 28 days or in a year, that's nobody's business but yours.

If you haven't done so already, I again invite you to buy or designate a spiral notebook as a spiritual journal. You may prefer, instead, to write your notes on a computer. If you are not comfortable with writing, you may choose to think through your responses to the "Thinking/ Journaling" segments—or say them aloud. Whatever connects you to the daily experiences and learnings is helpful. Remember to explore the feelings that come along with experience. If you can't do all of the exercises in a given day, do what you can.

Here's an introduction to the meditations and the exercises that are waiting for you. You may want to test-drive one, two, or all three.

MEDITATION PRACTICE

When you are ready, choose a time and a quiet place. Even a closet or a small space in the attic or the basement or out on the deck or in the back yard will do. If the only quiet place you can use is a bathroom, and no one will bother you there, try that. If your energy is wound so tight that you'd jump out of your skin if you tried to sit quietly for a few minutes, take a walk around the block. Jog in place. Do what it takes to release that energy. Free your mind to turn inward instead of thinking about what you should be doing, could be doing, will be doing, or don't want to do.

Ear plugs (the white, waxy kind found in grocery stores and drug stores) can be helpful if noise is a problem. If you live with others, let them know you want some meditation privacy and make sure they understand—or invite them to join you. Cell phones and other personal electronics should be turned off.

Soft music may be used to bring about a relaxed frame of mind. When you are ready to meditate, it's your choice, but it may be best to shut the music off to avoid distraction from your connection with soul mind.

Begin

- Sit quietly on a chair, feet flat on the floor, shoes off. Or sit on a cushion, back straight, in any comfortable position. Close your eyes. Rub the palms of your hands together briskly several times to help build energy for your meditation. This may create a light tingling sensation in the palms. Then, rest your hands, palms up, on your thighs. You may want to form a circle with the tips of the thumbs and the index fingers to help clear your mind.

- With eyes still closed, you may wish to raise them to focus on an imaginary dot—black or any other color—in the middle of your forehead. This can help keep your mind on track.

- Maintain a receptive attitude. Your body should feel relaxed. Keep your eyes focused on that dot. Gently connect with your innermost self. Allow all concerns, all thoughts to melt away.

- If the outer mind gets noisy, escort it offstage as necessary and return to your meditation. If you find yourself nodding off (which commonly happens at first when you slip into the relaxed space between wakefulness and sleep), bring your mind and your closed eyes back to that dot. Stay focused and receptive.

- Remain in meditation for a few minutes.

Finish

- To end your meditation, take a few gentle, deep breaths, open your eyes, and rejoin your outer life.

Exercise A. SEEING WITH FRESH EYES

I have found that my journal is as useful when I write down an opportunity missed as when I do things "right." It helps me to remember that I could have done better. It also helps me be on the lookout for similar situations later on. Someone has said, *"The past is dead and the future may never come. Today is a gift, which is why it's called the present."*

Look for the gift in the present of the following:

- *Spend part of a day deeply concentrating on the living world.* At some point, single out something that's alive (and not human) and focus on it to the exclusion of all else—just one thing. Make no judgments about its supposed material value. Notice its colors, its lines, and its textures. Be aware of the shadows it casts, the light it reflects. Sense its uniqueness. Open yourself to it fully.

- *Later, take a walk where you will see trees or some plants—* whatever the season. If that's impractical, focus on a plant you have around the house or a pet. Take the time to focus on Nature or the animal world.

Thinking/Journaling

You may want to make some notes in your journal on what you learned and how you felt during this exercise. Try not to judge your experiences as "good" or "bad."

Exercise B. HEARING WITH FRESH EARS

- *Wherever you are, spend five minutes focusing on everything you hear.* Notice if the sounds become more distinct as you pay attention to them. If closing your eyes helps for this exercise, do that. What kinds of sounds are you aware of? Does focusing on sounds help you to hear more layers of the "music" around you? How do you feel while doing this exercise?

- *Ask someone to talk to you about something that really interests him or her for a few minutes*—preferably something that you know little or nothing about. It could be a hobby, some aspect of politics, or how that person stays fit—whatever. Really listen. Ask follow-up questions—*"Can you tell me more about ____?" "What else do you know about ____?"* Keep the focus of the conversation on learning about that topic. Don't allow yourself to distract the speaker with your experiences that may relate in some way. This is not a conversation. It's a fact-finding mission.

Thinking/Journaling

In the hearing exercise, were you surprised by what you learned? In what way? Did you find yourself more—or less—interested in the topic than you expected?

Staying Open

Write down the following questions in your notebook:

- What automatically irritates me?

- What frustrates me?

- What little things can make me angry? What larger things can make me angry?

If you can think of a few simple answers to these questions, write them down. If you can't, bookmark the page in your journal and come back later when something does irritate, frustrate, or anger you—and fill in the spaces. Come back to this list occasionally to see if your attitudes change.

To benefit from the workbook, it's not necessary to believe everything you've read so far in *Streetwise Spirituality*. If you still have some doubts, fine. Carry them with you. When you're done with the program, you'll still be walking around, bumping into opportunities to learn, just like the rest of us in Earth School. Hopefully, though, you'll have a better handle on what's going on with you, and why.

Chapter Ten
Workbook: On Patience

*J*uggling traffic jams, people, jobs, hobbies, family, and everything in between—we have too much to do and too little time. We're always hearing (or saying), *"I have noooo patience."* We fidget while standing in line. We hate being put on hold. We sleep too little. Eight hours a night unconscious? *"I'll sleep when I'm dead!"* Caffeine is the fuel that keeps us going. And we wonder why life is just a blur. That's the way life is, the way it's supposed to be. Isn't it?

The lecturer described patience as a gateway concept, a foundation for learning other aspects of inner fitness. That's why 14 of the days of workbook practice focus on learning this life skill before we continue on to a week of perseverance and a week of adaptability. When I first began working with these materials, I wanted to discover if inner fitness could lead to greater strength, endurance, and flexibility at my core. It did, but not overnight.

The hard part was making patience relevant in a culture that has no use for it. Am I supposed to pretend I am unfazed when my computer gets sluggish, or the heel of my favorite pair of shoes breaks off? Do I paste on a Buddha-like smile while trying to wave down a taxi—when there are no taxis to be found? Who can be patient under pressure? And what does it matter, anyway? Gradually, I found my answers by examining how my expectations, fantasies, and attitudes had colored my lifescape as surely as sunsets paint the afternoon sky.

In this book, I have shared—and will share—how far I had to come so you can know how unlikely it is that you are standing any further down on the evolutionary ladder than I was. If I can succeed at making my life bloom, you can, too. You probably have a leg up on me already. Go on. Surpass me. My voice will cheer you on.

Patience: Day 1

MORNING
Begin with the meditation and intention (A), followed by the quotation (B), the life story (C), and the growth practice segment (D).

A. Meditation

1. *Invitation*

- Begin by rubbing your palms together briskly for a few seconds.

- Then, rest your hands, palms up, in your lap or on your thighs.

- You may wish to make a circle with thumb and forefinger with the remaining fingers relaxed to help focus your mind.

- Sit quietly for a few moments, eyes closed.

- With eyes still closed, you may wish to raise them to focus on an imaginary dot in the middle of your forehead. Maintain that focus for two or three minutes—throughout the meditation. Hold a receptive attitude.

2. *This Day's Intention*

- When you are ready to make an intention to act on throughout this day, think to yourself:
  I will not judge or criticize others.

- Repeat that thought:
  I will not judge or criticize others.

3. *Releasing and Relaxing*

- After a few moments, release your intention and rest in peaceful, receptive, inner connection for a few minutes. If the outer mind begins to chatter, send it gently on its way, focus on your breath, and return to your meditation.

4. *Return*

- When you are ready to end your meditation, take a couple of deep breaths, open your eyes, and bring yourself back to your outer life.

5. *Start the Day*

- With eyes open, say aloud:
  I will not judge or criticize others.

- You may put your intention on the fridge behind a magnet for this and all the following intentions. Or you may just want to repeat it to yourself as needed.

B. Quotation

We should be patient with what others do, even though we may not like it very much. We are not here to criticize or judge.

-The Lecturer

C. Life Story: *I, Judge and Jury*

For years, I thought—no, I *knew*—I was right. Politicians, corporate types, inside traders, petty crooks, and others I didn't like, didn't understand, and didn't respect were mercilessly judged and quickly dismissed. My worst criticisms were reserved, of course, for me. Nothing I did was ever good enough.

People who worked out at my club got judged if their workouts were less rigorous than mine. And then there were the women who arrived in full regalia—with heavy makeup, gorgeous hair done just so, and skin-tight clothing chosen for maximum impact and appeal—well, we know why they're at the club, don't we? I'd sniff at their lily-soft regimens while I, in my tattered, mismatched, faded, baggy gym clothes, streamed with righteous sweat!

After I became aware of how judgmentally I moved through the world, I saw it at the grocery store, where I glowered at parents whose brats yowled for candy. Waiting in line for a pump at the gas station, I fumed at people who didn't pay up—and get out of my way. What a shock it was to realize that just as the person in front of me was in *my* way, the person behind me had a "my way," too. Could my slow feet be irritating other people? No. Impossible. I'm the model of perfection. Just ask me!

The more conscious I became, the worse it got. Who did I think I was—God, maybe? I started questioning my automatic reactions. It was a surprise to see how often I not only judged situations and people, but *mis*judged them. I recall my irritation with a student who sat behind me in a class in college, driving me crazy with strange, loud clicking noises. Why didn't someone make her stop? Finally, I'd had enough. I whirled around—and saw that the young woman was blind. She was using a Braille writing device. She was punching the letters of her notes into cards she would later read with her fingers. I felt embarrassed, and of course I no longer judged her.

When I made a conscious effort not to judge others, I eased off on judging myself, too. If others weren't perfect, I didn't have to be. That was fortunate because I had always managed to disappoint myself in that area.

A friend of mine had a fall-off-the-flat-Earth moment the other day. Standing in line, she noticed a pair of slender men ahead of her. They were dressed in matching outfits—black leather jackets, pants, biker boots—complete with silver studs and chains. Hidden behind several other people, my friend stared at them. They were trying, and failing, to act like biker toughs. *"A pair of poofs,"* thought my friend. But then, one of the men turned just enough to show his profile. With a shock, she recognized her political science professor, a man who had given her the intellectual tools to sift through hype and half-truths. My friend had believed her mind was unbiased—but how easily ugly stereotypes and prejudice floated to its surface!

It had happened so quickly. The man she thought she knew had disappeared. Or had he? The man she laughed at wasn't funny anymore. Or was he?

D. Growth Practice

- Can you consciously keep an eye on any tendency to auto-matically judge others for how they dress, speak, or act? Try to see that everyone has a "my way" that's as important to them as yours is to you.

AFTERNOON

E. Thinking/Journaling

- Write about two experiences—once when you were criticized for something and once when you criticized someone else (either in your mind or verbally). Was either criticism justified? When I criticize someone else, it usually makes me feel superior to that person. Could you be feeling something similar? Can you think of a better way to deal with a tendency to automatically criticize?

EVENING

F. Consciousness Expansion

- Can you accept that everyone has a "my way"? Could someone else's "way" ever become more important to you than your own? What might it take for that to happen?

- Do you feel driven, never satisfied with what you do, always looking to the next challenge so you can throw yourself into it? What could you do to take yourself off the perfection hook, but still feel energized to do a good job?

G. Think About

Years ago, I had a friend who loved the poetry of Kahlil Gibran. When she discovered that he had lived an imperfect life, she discarded both the man and his poetry. Has your perception of someone else ever changed drastically because you came across an additional piece of information? Can we learn from someone else's wisdom without expecting that person to be anything other than human?

Good Night Meditation

Relax completely for a few minutes in silence, eyes closed. Ask yourself these questions: What did I learn today? What did I share with someone else? What could I have done better? How can I align myself more closely with my soul mind?

Patience: Day 2

MORNING
Start your day off with the meditation and intention (A), followed by the quotation (B), the life story (C), and the growth practice segment (D).

A. Meditation

1. *Invitation*

- Rub your palms together briskly for a few seconds.

- Then, rest your hands, palms up, in your lap or on your thighs.

- Make a circle with thumb and forefinger with the remaining fingers relaxed.

- Sit quietly for a few moments, eyes closed.

- With eyes still closed, raise them to focus on an imaginary small dot in the middle of your forehead. Maintain that focus throughout the meditation. Hold a receptive attitude. Do not worry about what it is that you receive.

2. *This Day's Intention*

- When you are ready to make your day-long intention, hold these words in mind:
  I will be patient with myself.

- Repeat that thought:
  I will be patient with myself.

3. *Releasing and Relaxing*

- After a few moments, release your intention and rest in peaceful, receptive inner connection for a minute or two. Release thoughts that may arise and return to your meditation.

4. *Return*

- When you are ready, take a couple of deep breaths, open your eyes, and bring yourself back to your outer life.

5. *Start the Day*

- With eyes open, say aloud:
  I will be patient with myself.

B. Quotation

When things go wrong, do you condemn or belittle yourself? We will understand our experiences better if we are patient with ourselves. Each experience is drawn to us for a purpose. Ask yourself, *"What can I learn from this?"*

–The Lecturer

C. Life Story: *Lost*

Wrapping up my final year of grad school at Columbia, I applied for a year-long Japanese language study fellowship at the former Stanford Center in Tokyo. In early September, a roundtrip ticket arrived. I packed my bags and confidently flew west.

In November, the Center wanted my tuition. *"Columbia sent the plane ticket,"* I said. *"Why ask me about money?"* No, I was told, the Center had paid for the ticket. Tuition had to come from Columbia. Frantic calls were made to New York, but no help was to be found. Shocked, angry, and confused, I left the Center.

I moved into a cheap Japanese-style rented room that measured a tiny nine feet by nine feet. By day, I taught English. At night, I wrote my Master's thesis. My typewriter sat on a low, Japanese-style table. Stacks of 3" x 5" index cards were everywhere—covered with vital scribbles about a long-dead Japanese educator/philosopher.

To make copies, I sandwiched sheets of messy carbon paper between sheets of typing paper. Mistakes were erased letter by letter, and typed over. If you weren't an excellent typist, which I wasn't, you spent hours erasing and retyping. And if you were impatient, which I was, you got irritated. The more irritated I became, the more mistakes I made.

Like most Japanese buildings, mine had neither central heat nor insulation. From December through March, I could watch snowflakes fall both outside the window and between the wooden slats that made up the outside walls of my second-story room. Tall kerosene heaters in an earthquake-prone city terrified me and I refused to buy one. My hands were usually blue with the cold, which did not improve typing accuracy or speed. After tearing yet another handful of paper and carbons out of the typewriter in mid-winter, I made a snap decision: I would type only the original! At the post office, I filled out a form that required someone at Columbia to sign for the thesis. What could go wrong?

After asking for a progress report months later, I learned that someone at the school had, indeed, signed for my thesis. No one could read the signature. And no one had ever seen my manuscript. I rewrote the thesis from scratch—making two copies—and it was quickly accepted.

A Master's in Japanese philosophy does not qualify you to make a living. It's only a necessary step toward a PhD, the "union card" required to cling to the bottom teaching rung at a university. Eighteen months of painful challenges in Japan after five years of unrelenting academic pressure back home tipped me over. All I wanted now was to coast, preferably in Japan.

Tired of blaming the nameless person who lost my first thesis, I turned my anger on myself. I was the one whose impatience destroyed my dream of university teaching. My sleepless head was filled with "should-haves" and "could-have-beens." Self-hatred, I finally understood, accomplished nothing. It only left me charred, hollowed out, adrift.

In time, I let it all go. I realized that we all make mistakes. Every one of us. Some do it a little more spectacularly than others, but in our capacity to make our ships wobble, bobble, and threaten to sink to the bottom of the sea, we are all brothers and sisters.

D. Growth Practice

- Will you extend your intention to practice patience with yourself to patience with someone else today—especially when you don't feel like it?

AFTERNOON

E. Thinking/Journaling

Choose one of the following to write about:

- Was there ever a time that you made a snap decision without thinking it through to its logical conclusion—and paid dearly for it? What was that about? If you could relive that experience, what would you do differently and why?

- Can you recall beating yourself up over what you should have done, could have done, or would have done if circumstances had been different? Write a paragraph about your own relationship with the three wicked witches, "Shoulda," "Woulda," and "Coulda."

EVENING

F. Consciousness Expansion

- Carpenters say, *"Measure twice. Cut once."* We can't always do an A+ job—and not everything demands that kind of attention to quality. What about those projects that do require it? Do you habitually cut too many corners in your rush to meet too many deadlines? If that's the case, would you like to make some changes?

G. Think About

I have repeated the same kinds of mistakes all my life because I refused to learn from them. When we lose what we most desire to keep—jobs, relationships, etc.,—life seems unfair. Try to remember that lessons come in all forms and a crisis is an invitation from your soul mind to grow. For most of us, that invitation is hard to recognize while we are in pain, but it lies there in the darkness.

> √ *Look back. Have you been able to mentally switch places with a person who has a "my way" that's different from yours—maybe someone behind you at the checkout counter or in traffic? How did that feel?*

Good Night Meditation

Relax completely for a few minutes in silence, eyes closed. Ask yourself: What did I learn today? What did I share with someone else? What could I have done better? How can I align myself more closely with my soul mind?

Patience: Day 3

MORNING
Start your day off with A, B, C, and D.

A. Meditation

1. Invitation

- Rub your palms together briskly for a few seconds.

- Then, rest your hands, palms up, in your lap or on your thighs.

- Make a circle with thumb and forefinger with the remaining fingers relaxed.

- Sit quietly for a few moments, eyes closed.

- With eyes still closed, raise them to focus on an imaginary small dot in the middle of your forehead. Maintain that focus throughout the meditation. Hold a receptive attitude.

2. This Day's Intention

- When you are ready to make your day-long intention, think to yourself:
  I will be patient with other people.

- Repeat that thought:
  I will be patient with other people.

3. Releasing and Relaxing

- After a few moments, release your intention and rest in peaceful, receptive inner connection for a minute or two. Release thoughts that may arise and come back to your meditation.

4. Return

- When you are ready, take a couple of deep breaths, open your eyes, and return to your outer life.

5. Start the Day

- With eyes open, say aloud:
  I will be patient with other people.

B. Quotation

> Patience with oneself and patience with others is connected.
> One cannot exist without the other. Only after you have truly
> mastered patience with yourself will you understand what you
> see when you interact with other people. Know that the same God
> that moves one moves all.
>
> —The Lecturer

C. Life Story: *Living Others' Lives*

I have long tried to live others' lives for them—especially when friends had boyfriend troubles. From my ivory tower of the Knowledge of All Things Romantic, I'd calmly advise, *"We should pick guys who are about 95% of what we already want them to be. Your boyfriend's at maybe 20%. Dump him."* They never did. Why not? Why wouldn't they let go of the drama? Change the attitude? Stop expecting miracles?

I rarely looked to myself for advice, though, which makes me think of Elaine, Cory's lady friend. Cory was a bright, shy violinist I'd met in college. Elaine was generous, funny, and lively—an appealing mix of qualities. She had a great British accent, a dry wit, and a wonderfully tweedy look. She also had a low boredom threshold. Wherever we went—to a party or just walking around downtown—Elaine's brown eyes would eventually lose their focus. It was like watching the curtain ring down in the middle of a play. *"Right,"* she'd say, *"We're off."* And we'd be gone.

At a party once, Elaine stood up, towering over those of us who were strewn around the living room on low furniture. *"We're off,"* she announced. She expected Cory and me to be, as always, right behind her. We weren't. Well, *I* wasn't. I was deep in conversation with a twinkly eyed, dark-haired man who held promise. I stayed put, chatting with my "potential," sipping my wine, and reaching for another chunk of cheese. Cory looked at Elaine's retreating back and then at me. I shrugged my shoulders. He caught up with her and whispered something. She stared at me in astonishment. I gave her a toothy grin. She sat down, eyes wide, back straight. In ten minutes, she was out the door. We followed.

I felt angry every time Elaine played her game—which was actually *our* game. I never told her that. Maybe we could have used our differences to learn how to exercise patience with one another—and perhaps we would have grown closer in the process. What would have happened if I'd said, *"Elaine, can we discuss this? I don't feel ready to leave yet. Why don't we stay for another, say, 30 minutes? Does that work for you?"* That way, she wouldn't have gotten everything she wanted (leaving now) and I wouldn't have gotten everything I wanted (staying for another hour). The friendship, though, might have deepened through talking our differences out. Neither Elaine nor I knew how to be part of a pair. Instead, we made one-sided decisions and expected others to go along with them. Communication based on the courage to express feelings and the patience to listen to things we might not want to hear was a foreign concept.

A year after Cory and Elaine moved away, I realized that part of the reason her actions irritated me was that, down deep, we were twins. I, too, wanted parties to be over when I said they were. I believed that friendships were preserved, however, by keeping your mouth shut—until you couldn't. When I reached the point where I was ready to explode, I'd find an excuse to break the friendship off. It never occurred to me that both parties could win if both exercised a little patience, a little courage, and a willingness to bend a bit. Instead, I set myself up to lose repeatedly with strong-willed friends—until I "won" by discarding them. Seems so silly now. Just when we could have grown closer, I'd walk out the door. I wonder if it wasn't closeness that I feared—and sabotaged.

D. Growth Practice

- If you've had problems with someone recently, try to think about the situation from that person's perspective. Is it possible to bring patience to bear on the situation? Could both of you give up something you want to find a reasonable compromise, one that would nourish the relationship?

AFTERNOON

E. Thinking/Journaling

- Write about your past history with a friend and/or a romantic partner, one with communication problems. Write about how patience might have helped create a better outcome. Can you find any "shoulds" in operation here?

EVENING

F. Consciousness Expansion

- Do you hold back your real thoughts from someone special in your life? Why? Would you like to change that approach? What might you like to share—and when?

G. Think About

When I think back, almost none of my "good advice" to friends has ever been taken. When I put the shoe on the other foot, I immediately understand. I don't really like getting advice from other people—not about my private life, anyway. Job advice? Sure. Boyfriend advice? Never. *"What?"* I would think. *"Do these people believe they can live my life for me?"*

√ *Look back: How are you doing with letting go of criticism of yourself and other people?*

Good Night Meditation

Relax completely for a few minutes in silence, eyes closed. Ask yourself: What did I learn today? What did I share with another? What could I have improved on? How can I bring myself into better alignment with my soul mind?

Patience: Day 4

MORNING
Please do A, B, C, and D.

A. Meditation

1. *Invitation*

- Rub your palms together briskly for a few seconds.

- Then, rest your hands, palms up, in your lap or on your thighs.

- Make a circle with thumb and forefinger with the remaining fingers relaxed.

- Sit quietly for a few moments, eyes closed.

- With eyes still closed, raise them to focus on an imaginary small dot in the middle of your forehead. Maintain that focus throughout the meditation. Hold a receptive attitude.

2. *This Day's Intention*

- When you are ready to make a day-long intention, think to yourself:
  Patience helps me to understand.

- Repeat that thought:
  Patience helps me to understand.

3. *Releasing and Relaxing*

- After a few moments, release your intention and rest in peaceful, receptive inner connection for three or four minutes. Release any thoughts and return to your meditation.

4. *Return*

- When you are ready, take a couple of deep breaths, open your eyes, and bring yourself to full consciousness of where you are.

5. *Start the Day*

- With eyes open, say aloud:
  Patience helps me to understand.

B. Quotation

With patience comes understanding.

-The Lecturer

C. Life Story: *Off Camera*

My favorite job during 11 years in Japan was as a newscaster and talk show host for Japan Cable Television—JCTV. That job also led me to a husband, but first things first.

The national hobby in Japan at that time was English conversation. As a "voice talent," I recorded many scripts written to help the Japanese brush up their conversation skills. At one recording session, I met a tall, wickedly funny redhead. During the pre-recording voice tests, Candace told me she'd just been hired as a newscaster at Japan Cable Television. *"I'd give* anything *to do what you do,"* I sighed. She winked and told me to watch the English-language newspaper want ads—that's how she had found her job. Six months later, that's how I got mine.

Candace and I became close friends, talking by phone for hours every week. We rarely saw each other because we worked at the studio on alternate nights—and she lived a 90-minute train ride out of town.

Two years later, Candace decided to move back to the States and file for divorce. Before she left, she asked if I'd join her for lunch in the city, and that was how I met her husband. Candace was radiant that day. It was the glow people get when everything seems possible, when we are ready to leave heartache behind and start over fresh. I felt hopeful for her. Back then, I, too, thought I could instantly revamp my life by changing my circumstances, my location, or my man.

After lunch, Candace turned to us. *"You know,"* she said, *"you two would make a perfect couple. You're so much alike."* I stared at her while her husband looked down, trying not to cry.

That's what happened. He was lonely. I was lonely. We married a year later. I was incapable of being patient at the time—not with myself and certainly not with Stu. I wanted everything to be perfect, perfect in the way I wanted it to be, and to stay that way. Forever. Patience might have taught me to appreciate Stu for what he was and to work toward a good life for us both until death we did part.

Instead, I kept trying to change him. I was never satisfied. And now

I know why. Beneath my desire to recreate him was a deeper desire. I wanted him to stay the same—in love with Candace and permanently beyond my reach. While he was still crazy about her, that hurt—and fueled the flames. It was pure drama. Eventually, Stu did turn to me in love. My fire cooled. And went out.

Stu had patience. He'd learned to ride through the day-to-day difficulties that came up in a relationship, and not lose sight of the fundamental connection. He understood how to let petty annoyances go while I clung to them, putting each one lovingly into my ever-expanding gunnysack. I understood nothing about love as a long-term process. After the fireworks died, what else could there be? Exactly what might keep two people together, other than inertia?

After eight years of marriage, Stu said we had become like two old shoes together. He had found a comfortable groove and was happy to have his life move alongside mine. The image seemed to give him a sense of contentment. It made my feet itch for some other place, some other time, some other life.

D. Growth Practice

- Today, consider taking a walk while thinking about three people who've been helping you understand important truths about life. Consider thanking them if such a discussion will not cause any of them pain.

AFTERNOON

E. Thinking/Journaling

- Have you ever thought that by moving from one place to another, your life would be improved? What about trying to find happiness by getting rid of one relationship and starting a new one—or starting a new one while you're still in the old one? What's that about? Write a couple of paragraphs around the questions here that most speak to you. What have you learned?

EVENING

F. Consciousness Expansion

- Have you ever hurt your chances for happiness by wanting everything to be perfect?

G. Think About

Every relationship goes through its courtship phase, and then it changes. We all feel good in the excitement of the moment while the other person seems to be the answer to every prayer. What can we do when the fireworks die down or go out? What might patience have to do with it and what would that look like on a day-to-day basis? What about mutual respect? What about the courage to look within? Could the keys to what may be pulling us away from one another lie in our unrealistic expectations?

Good Night Meditation

Relax completely for a few minutes in silence, eyes closed. Ask yourself: What did I learn today? What did I share with another? What could I have improved on? How can I bring myself into better alignment with my soul mind?

Patience: Day 5

MORNING
Please do A, B, C, and D.

A. Meditation

1. *Invitation*

- Rub your palms together briskly for a few seconds.

- Then, rest your hands, palms up, in your lap or on your thighs.

- Make a circle with thumb and forefinger with the remaining fingers relaxed.

- Sit quietly for a few moments, eyes closed.

- With eyes still closed, raise them to focus on an imaginary small dot in the middle of your forehead. Maintain that focus throughout the meditation. Hold a receptive attitude.

2. *This Day's Intention*

- When you are ready to make a day-long intention, think to yourself:
  I will use patience to connect with others.

- Repeat that thought:
  I will use patience to connect with others.

3. *Releasing and Relaxing*

- After a few moments, release your intention and rest in peaceful, receptive inner connection for three or four minutes. Release thoughts that may arise.

4. *Return*

- When you are ready, take a couple of deep breaths, open your eyes, and bring yourself to full consciousness of where you are.

5. *Start the Day*

- With eyes open, say aloud:
  I will use patience to connect with others.

B. Quotation

Patience connects us.   −The Lecturer

C. Life Story: *Like Magic*

Stu and I were living parallel lives—he went to the office and I went to the TV studio. We worked long hours and had little time together. And when we were at home, he did his thing and I did mine. Maybe because so much divided us, we created a common bond by organizing a charitable group. We looked for volunteers among the congregations of the five English-speaking churches in Tokyo. Only one person stepped forward—Michiko, a young, smiling Japanese college grad. Her English was excellent, so we knew she wasn't looking to use us for language practice. She really wanted to help.

We received a request for a visit from a facility for severely handicapped Japanese. One Saturday, the three of us traveled by train past miles of brown winter fields that lay under gray winter skies. Within minutes of our arrival, a round-faced, red-cheeked boy—the caretaker's son—came running to meet us. He explained that our group had been singled out because some of the residents were learning conversational English. They wanted to practice on native speakers. Michiko said she'd play along—speaking only English when spoken to.

Our ten-minute walk brought us to a sprawling gray concrete box of a building. The boy took us to a conference room with three tables. Seated at each table were two or three residents. Stu, Michiko, and I were invited to sit—with one English-speaker per table.

I sat to the left of a young wheelchair-bound man. His head was canted severely to the left and twisted slightly backwards. His left arm was held birdlike at his side, the hand a fixed claw. The right arm was a little more under his control.

I had been raised to be sympathetic toward the disabled, but my daily world had nothing but able-bodied people in it. Feeling trapped in a situation outside my experience and possibly beyond my ability to handle, I kept acting as if we were having a "normal" conversation. This was no normal situation.

The young man kept his eyes fixed on me as I filled the air with pleasantries more suited to a garden party. Then, he began to talk—and talk. And it was all in *Japanese*! I could read Japanese. I spoke it poorly.

I swiveled my head around, trying to spot the boy who'd brought us from the station. I saw only tables with disabled people in conversation with Stu or Michiko. I needed a translator! The young man continued softly talking, his phrases breaking up, his words stretching out. I considered bolting from the room in search of someone who could translate. I knew that was too rude—even for an American.

At that moment, my brain registered something familiar. I heard, *"My—xxxx—is—xxxxx."* I looked at the young man. He repeated the phrase, slowly. *"My—name—is—Ichiro. What—is—xxx—name?"* He was speaking *English,* not Japanese. He had been speaking English all along! When I finally gave him my full attention, the sounds started to make sense. The more I listened, the more I understood.

As our conversation slowly progressed, Ichiro explained that at the age of 18, he'd been in a car accident. No one in his family had the time to give him the one-on-one care he needed. So he came here. *"Does your family visit you?"* I asked. *"No,"* he said. *"They—never—come. They—are—too—busy."*

I never saw Ichiro again. Soon after that, I moved to Los Angeles. I haven't forgotten the young man who was so patient and so determined to connect with me that he overcame my almost equally strong and impatient desire to disconnect from him.

D. Growth Practice

- Today, connect with someone with whom you've had some communications difficulties. Can you find a "should" here? Try being patient with that person and with yourself. Take a walk in Nature at lunch if you can.

AFTERNOON

E. Thinking /Journaling

- Write about your attitudes toward those of a different sexual orientation, ethnicity, or physical ability from you. Have any of your ideas about them changed over time? If they have, how have they changed? Why?

EVENING

F. Consciousness Expansion

- It's normal to be uncomfortable in unfamiliar situations. How would you hope to use nervousness in an unfamiliar situation to connect, rather than disconnect?

G. Think About

Try to stay open to the thought that we may be able to learn even from those who seemingly have nothing to teach us.

Good Night Meditation

Relax completely for a few minutes in silence, eyes closed. Ask yourself: What did I learn today? What did I share with another? What could I have improved on? How can I bring myself into better alignment with my soul mind?

Patience: Day 6

MORNING
Experience A, B, C, and D.

A. Meditation

1. *Invitation*

- Rub your palms together briskly for a few seconds.

- Then, rest your hands, palms up, in your lap or on your thighs.

- Make a circle with thumb and forefinger with the remaining fingers relaxed.

- Sit quietly for a few moments, eyes closed.

- With eyes still closed, raise them to focus on an imaginary small dot in the middle of your forehead. Maintain that focus throughout the meditation. Hold a receptive attitude.

2. *This Day's Intention*

- When you are ready to make a day-long intention, think to yourself:
  I will be mellow, no matter what.

- Repeat that thought:
  I will be mellow, no matter what.

3. *Releasing and Relaxing*

- After a few moments, release your intention and rest in peaceful, receptive inner connection for three or four minutes. Release thoughts of past or future that may arise and return to your meditation.

4. *Return*

- When you are ready, take a couple of deep breaths, open your eyes, and bring yourself to full consciousness of where you are.

5. *Start the Day*

- With eyes open, say aloud:
  I will be mellow, no matter what.

B. Quotation

> It's easy to be mellow and harmonious when there is no reason to be anything else. We forget to be patient when it's most needed.
> —The Lecturer

C. Life Story: *For Nothing*

Stu and I had moved to West Hollywood, California, while I tried to figure out how to break into the American TV news market. I came home from my journalism classes at the University of Southern California one afternoon to a jammed-open underground garage door. Seeing nothing out of the ordinary, I drove inside and parked the Camaro.

My mind full of the day's events, I opened the car door and put one foot on the concrete garage floor. That's when I met a tall, slim man with a gun. He shoved his body between the door and me, blocking escape. *"Don't scream,"* he said. I, of course, began filling the car with defiant yowls. The man reached for my purse. I automatically threw it against the far door while continuing to deafen us both. He aimed the gun at my face with his left hand. He then punched me on the jaw with his right, stopping my screams. Reaching over me and hooking the purse strap through his fingers, he ran.

When I stumbled out of the garage, I saw the thief crouched behind a hedge, pawing through my purse. *My* purse! I pointed accusingly at him and began screaming again. He took off. I chased after him down the street. He slipped into the darkness of an open garage. I started to follow. At that moment, self-preservation kicked in. I stopped just outside the garage—still screaming and pointing. Two men in a passing car asked what was wrong. *"That man in the garage stole my purse!"* I shouted. The thief soon sprinted out of the garage, right toward me. I stared at him, remembering that he had a gun. And I stopped screaming. He brushed roughly past me and kept on running. This time, though, I didn't chase him.

The detective who wrote the case up later said that the thief never intended to kill me—because I gave him every excuse to do so.

The experience shocked and frightened me because of my reaction. Someone I did not know lived at the heart of me. She was as ferocious as a lioness, but she had no fangs or claws—only a scream. I took a self-defense course six weeks later. If you don't have opportunities to jam a heel into a man's instep or smash him in the Adam's apple, you gradually forget the finer points. But I imagine I could improvise.

All this happened when I still believed a woman had to walk through the world coated in sugar. I had chained down my inner raging bitch so tightly that I didn't even recognize her when she rose up, ready to wage all-out battle over a small injustice.

Looking back, there was a larger lesson. People often died violently in southern California during chump-change robberies. My "should" in operation was that no one had the right to take what's mine. I would have died only because I was out of control, completely unconscious of the potential results of my actions. And the only appropriate epitaph would have been: *"Here lies Carol. Died on autopilot. For nothing."*

If I had it to do over again, I'd look at the experience as a kind of business transaction. I had what he wanted—money. In exchange for my money, he would hand me my life. Although there are situations where it's appropriate to fight back, in this case, I should have kept my mouth shut, given him the purse, and been grateful I could still breathe when it was all over.

D. Growth Practice

- Stay on the lookout for automatic angry, irritated, or frustrated reactions to your circumstances today. Try to weigh each situation consciously and respond in a way that is appropriate to the moment—which may not be the way you automatically want to react.

AFTERNOON

E. Thinking/Journaling

- What can get you going—politics, religion, the economy, ecology, other people's (bad) choices? Pick a topic that makes your heart beat a little faster. It's important to invite your feeling self to participate in this exercise. Purely intellectual exercises of this sort don't involve enough of our complete selves to teach us much. In this exercise, practice debating with yourself. Write down three arguments that back up your favorite opinion about something. Then, take the opposite side and make another three arguments that are equally strong. Write a few sentences about how this exercise in shifting your perspective makes you feel.

EVENING

F. Consciousness Expansion

- In a society where "cool" is a positive attribute, private feelings are not often shown in public, and we may even learn to cut ourselves off from them. Some people get so good at this that they lose track of their feelings altogether. Emotions can lie in wait, ready to leap forth when we feel cheated, mistreated, disempowered, or in danger. Just like fear short-circuits our thinking, automatic anger can keep us from weighing all of our options and choosing a response that fits the circumstances. Or we may have programmed ourselves to let dark emotions out only at people who can't fight back—clerks, toll road workers, the people we see on television, or "them." Give yourself a break. Find something or someone that predictably pulls your chain—and don't allow it. Rise above it—just for fun.

G. Think About

Think through the steps of how you could face a robbery consciously, based on your most important goal (staying alive) in the face of fear or anger. What if someone told you to get into the trunk of a car? What if someone wanted your car? Do you know that running away from someone with a gun in a zigzag manner reduces the chances of getting shot?

Good Night Meditation

Relax completely for a few minutes in silence, eyes closed. Ask yourself: What did I learn today? What did I share with another? What could I have improved on? How can I bring myself into better alignment with my soul mind?

Patience: Day 7

MORNING
Use A, B, C, and D to begin your day.

A. Meditation

1. *Invitation*

- Rub your palms together briskly for a few seconds.

- Then, rest your hands, palms up, in your lap or on your thighs.

- Make a circle with thumb and forefinger with the remaining fingers relaxed.

- Sit quietly for a few moments, eyes closed.

- With eyes still closed, raise them to focus on an imaginary small dot in the middle of your forehead. Maintain that focus throughout the meditation. Hold a receptive attitude.

2. *This Day's Intention*

- When you are ready to make a day-long intention, think to yourself:
  I will forgive.

- Repeat that thought:
  I will forgive.

3. *Releasing and Relaxing*

- After a few moments, release your intention and rest in peaceful, receptive inner connection for a few minutes. Release any thoughts that come up and return to your meditation.

4. *Return*

- When you are ready, take a couple of deep breaths, open your eyes, and bring yourself to full consciousness of where you are.

5. *Start the Day*

- With eyes open, say aloud:
  I will forgive.

B. Quotation

> We know that other people are here to learn, just as we have learned, and just as we are learning. If they fail to come up to what we call our standards, be patient. Forgive them, for they know not what they do. This has been said in the past. It's as true today as it was back then. That understanding will fill us with a sense of patience. And peace.
>
> —The Lecturer

C. Life Story: *Kindest Cut*

For many years, I typically had one best friend—everyone else was an acquaintance. People, I found, could not give you a hard time if they didn't know you very well. So my guard was down when a casual acquaintance handed me my severed head one afternoon—with complete indifference.

I met Angie through a northern Virginia entrepreneurs' club. Her short blonde hair was always salon-perfect, her makeup and clothes stunning and stylish on her trim body. Angie ran an art gallery her wealthy husband had bought for her.

We were standing at a conference for small businesses. I was, as usual, eyeing the men, wondering if any of them might be "the one." Angie and her husband had met when he got lost and rang her doorbell, looking for directions. Keeping my eyes on the parade of men at the conference, I mentioned that I wouldn't mind finding a wealthy man. Angie's head flipped elegantly in my direction. *"To attract a man of substance, you'd have to have something to offer."* Her look said I was living in a dream world. We continued to cross paths after that, but we never exchanged another word. I didn't want to and she, no doubt, couldn't have cared less.

At that time, I was failing to make a living at selling a multi-level product no one had heard of. It was more than that. What I grabbed in the closet was what I wore. My habitually wayward hair got little attention. I had long believed that I should—and would—be judged solely by my intelligence. Angie didn't care about my brain or my fascinating past. She couldn't see either one. She saw what the world saw.

What did I have to offer? I had no meaningful work, no prospects, no sense of style that would identify me as acceptable to the world of business, no goals, and no guiding life principles. I had no talent at small talk. I was self-absorbed and unwilling to bend. As tall as I was, I was hard to miss. I was never noticed by any man that I wanted to be noticed by. And I was totally focused not on what I had to offer, but on what someone else—especially a man—could offer *me.*

I could not forgive Angie for leaving me no place to hide. For years, I feigned intense disinterest when a mutual friend shared news about Angie's life. All her successes reminded me of my failures. It wasn't until I could admit the truth of her words that the process of forgiveness began—a process I recognized when her name no longer brought up an automatic angry reaction.

D. Growth Practice

- Today, smile at someone you would usually not smile at, thinking, *"I wish for you what you most dearly want for yourself."* Do something for someone for no special reason. Give yourself a gift without a price tag: How about a walk? Or a long tub bath tonight?

AFTERNOON

E. Thinking/Journaling

Choose one of the following:

- Has anyone ever said or written something to you or about you that was extremely painful? Was there a useful lesson in it? Write a paragraph about that.
- If you could change a communication you had once with someone—a communication that was hurtful—how would you do that? Have you ever considered asking that person for forgiveness? Can you forgive yourself?

EVENING

F. Consciousness Expansion

- What small change could you make in yourself, a change that you think would result in a positive improvement in your life over time? Will you try it? Does it have anything to do with a "should"?

G. Think About

The lecturer said that shyness is rooted in the outer mind. I thought that shyness was like having blue eyes or brown. But he was right. Outer mind separates us from each other. It can make us feel cut off and uncomfortable in the company of strangers.

Outer mind is deeply involved in friendships that never get much beyond the basic need we humans have to spend time with each other. But what about the inner circle? More and more, I look for friends who nourish the deepest part of me. In the name of mutual growth, I have to be willing to voice some of my dark-side fears and failings—the areas I'm working on—to connect at a deep, meaningful level. I must choose well, trusting that my inner-circle friends will not use such knowledge to hurt or judge me. I must be a trustworthy vessel for their shadows, too. The philosopher Descartes said that everything excellent is as difficult as it is rare. Could that hold true for inner-circle friendships, too?

Good Night Meditation

Relax completely for a few minutes in silence, eyes closed. Ask yourself: What did I learn today? What did I share with another? What could I have improved on? How can I bring myself into better alignment with my soul mind?

Patience: Day 8

MORNING
Learn from A, B, C, and D.

A. Meditation

1. *Invitation*

- Rub your palms together briskly for a few seconds.
- Then, rest your hands, palms up, in your lap or on your thighs.
- Make a circle with thumb and forefinger with the remaining fingers relaxed.
- Sit quietly for a few moments, eyes closed.
- With eyes still closed, raise them to focus on an imaginary small dot in the middle of your forehead. Maintain that focus for five or six minutes. Hold a receptive attitude.

2. *This Day's Intention*

- When you are ready to shift into making your intention, think to yourself:
  I will be patient when my ideas are challenged.
- Repeat that thought:
  I will be patient when my ideas are challenged.

3. *Releasing and Relaxing*

- After a few moments, release your intention and rest in peaceful, receptive inner connection for a few minutes. Release any thoughts that come up and return to your meditation.

4. *Return*

- When you are ready, take a couple of deep breaths, open your eyes, and bring yourself to full consciousness of where you are.

5. *Start the Day*

- With eyes open, say aloud:
  I will be patient when my ideas are challenged.

B. Quotation

> *Most of us find it very difficult to exercise patience and tolerance when people challenge our ideas, or when situations require us to do something we don't want to do.*
>
> —The Lecturer

C. Life Story: *Just Do It*

When I started working this program, I decided to use the situations that irritated me as consciousness guideposts—instead of impatiently dismissing them (as was my habit). The idea sounded promising—but I was not ready for what I found.

Ever since I can remember, I've disliked being told what to do. One of my favorite words is "autonomous." Being self-directed is my idea of the good life. For example, I really, *really* disliked having to take notes at a meeting as the "secretary." Writers take notes. I take them all the time. I take them for *me*. Taking notes precise enough to become a set of minutes means I'm too busy writing to do much thinking. I *like* to think. I *like* to participate. I don't like being a pen-wielding mammal. When I read what the lecturer said about getting upset over having to do what we don't want to do, that seemed like a good place to start.

He also said there's no such thing as "menial work," work that is beneath us. *"There is only* work.*"* And it's not the work itself that's important. It's the way we treat it. When we allow ourselves to get ticked off about something we have to do, it doesn't matter how good the results are. We've already polluted them with our negative attitude, our anger. The lesson, he said, lies in our response—in whatever spirit of service we bring to the task. Arrogance had no place in a life well lived. Oh, I definitely had resisted learning *that* lesson!

An organization I belong to has a meeting every month. As an officer, I have no choice about attending meetings. Just recently, the usual note-taker had a scheduling conflict. Would I take her place? Not if I could help it! I tried very hard to find a substitute secretary and couldn't. I would have to take those notes, like it or not.

I walked into the meeting, keeping a close eye on my emotions. Was I feeling put upon? No. Angry? No. I was in neutral and worked hard to stay conscious. Listening carefully, I made detailed notes.

No matter what it sounds like, I had not grown wings. This turnaround happened because I had stumbled badly three months earlier. Funny how life always gives us another chance to learn what we didn't learn earlier.

Unexpectedly drafted into taking notes at a committee meeting late last year, I felt the familiar burn in the gut. Although I did what I had to, I definitely did not like it—as my face and body language told the room.

I find it's always harder to respond in a conscious manner when something comes at me with no chance to prepare for it. Sure enough, my unconscious outer mind took charge and I danced to the same old song with the same old steps for the same old reasons that have kept me dancing in the same old way forever.

So that's why I decided to stay conscious the next time this issue came up. And what do you know? It worked. Unconscious habit did not rule the day. I ruled the day—that inner I. People thanked me for compiling such an all-encompassing set of minutes. I smiled. They couldn't know the real challenge. It wasn't the minutes.

D. Growth Practice

- Try to maintain a conscious, accepting attitude today in response to whatever you are asked to do, especially if it comes as an unpleasant surprise.

AFTERNOON

E. Thinking/Journaling

Choose one of the following:

- Can you think of the last time that you felt frustrated when someone changed your plans for you? Did you react on automatic or respond consciously? Write about your experience.

- Can you remember having an experience that you did not handle well—and then having the opportunity to face something similar later on? How well did you do under pressure? If you can't remember such a situation, keep your eyes open for this to happen in the future—maybe on the road or in a store or when you feel you have too little time to accomplish something you want to accomplish.

EVENING

F. Consciousness Expansion

- If you must do things you don't like—pay bills, gather documents at tax time, or go food shopping, for example—see how patiently and consciously you can approach one of your least favorite repetitive situations the next time it comes up.

G. Think About

The outer mind is always ready to take over. I'm very familiar with mine. I had one boss tell me he'd be a lot happier if I learned to say "please" and "thank you." I was insulted. I was his equal! Why should I bow to him? Truth was, I wasn't his equal. I didn't sign his paychecks. He did sign mine. And so I learned to say "please" and "thank you." I resented it the entire time I worked for him. Now, I look back and wonder what I was thinking. These days, "please" and "thank you" come naturally and genuinely. Can you locate a place in your life where your outer mind still trips you up more frequently than you would like it to?

Good Night Meditation

Close your eyes and relax completely for a few minutes. Ask: What did I learn today? What did I share with another? What could I have improved on? How can I bring myself into greater alignment with my soul mind?

Patience: Day 9

MORNING
Try looking for the lessons in A, B, C, and D.

A. Meditation

1. *Invitation*

- Rub your palms together briskly for a few seconds.

- Then, rest your hands, palms up, in your lap or on your thighs.

- Make a circle with thumb and forefinger with the remaining fingers relaxed.

- Sit quietly for a few moments, eyes closed.

- With eyes still closed, raise them to focus on an imaginary small dot in the middle of your forehead. Maintain that focus for five or six minutes. Hold a receptive attitude.

2. *This Day's Intention*

- When you are ready to shift into making your intention, think to yourself:
  I will patiently learn my lessons.

- Repeat that thought:
  I will patiently learn my lessons.

3. *Releasing and Relaxing*

- After a few moments, release your intention and rest in peaceful, receptive inner connection for a few minutes. Release any thoughts that come up and return to your meditation.

4. *Return*

- When you are ready, take a couple of deep breaths, open your eyes, and bring yourself to full consciousness of where you are.

5. *Start the Day*

- With eyes open, say aloud:
  I will patiently learn my lessons.

B. Quotation

> We cannot escape our lessons just by impatiently pushing them aside.
>   —The Lecturer

C. Life Story: *Comets*

I long believed that we are truly alive only at peak moments. I couldn't stand quiet times. Instead of accepting them as part of life, I impatiently filled them. I'd turn on the TV, eat something I shouldn't, or get lost in e-mails. All of my distractions were mental or physical, never spiritual. All of them were bad for me, or at least not especially good. Sound familiar?

If every experience was not only meaningful, but inescapably mine to deal with, maybe I could no longer focus only on the "good stuff." Maybe the bad stuff, the dull stuff, the irritating and the ugly stuff all had a part to play—maybe.

I decided to focus on what was going on inside me when I started to get bored or down—instead of going on automatic. Sometimes, I discovered it was just my body telling me to stop living in my head so much. I listened—and ran down to the club for workouts. That surprised and pleased my body. It thanked me by starting to sprout muscles and burn flab.

Harder to deal with than boredom, though, were all my love dramas. You may wonder what patience has to do with love. As a matter of fact, a lot. I had met legions of exquisitely inappropriate men through the years. It was as if I'd written an ad: *"Tall, auburn-haired, green-eyed woman looking for life partner. Only loners incapable of love need apply."* Some prince was supposed to recognize me for the jewel I was, take me away, fill my life with romance, and solve all my problems. Sound childish? Sure does. That's where I lived.

So, if men were part of my curriculum, how could I use these "love" experiences for learning and growing, instead of moving inevitably from adoration to disenchantment, despair, anger, silence, and painful breakup?

Patience required a different approach. I had to assume men were there for reasons that went well beyond brown eyes or green, a cute smile, and a yummy set of broad shoulders (my weakness, I admit). I could see that their mission in life had never been to make me miserable. Maybe if I stopped impatiently leaping from lover to lover, trying to find someone perfect, and started looking for the lessons in the relationships, I could get off the merry-go-round. And go find the real thing.

At this point, my yammering mental commentator asked, *"What would you do with the real thing? Could you love a man who didn't hurt you?"* Oh, probably not. *"And what would it be like to be loved by such a man?"* Maybe boring. Too predictable. And the hardest question of all: *"Could a man like that love you as you are?"* Not likely. In my eyes, I had only two responsibilities toward lovers: First, I had to look a lot better the rest of the day than I did first thing in the morning. A dab of mascara and a smear of lipstick took care of that. Second, I had to be sweet, which meant being what he wanted me to be. That lasted until I saw him for what he really was—an ordinary guy—and started being what *I* really was, which wasn't what he bargained for.

A picture began to emerge. Old expectations about men had drawn these comets to crash unerringly, one after another, on the beach of my life. I had to face the truth. At root, all my guys were the same—different faces, different names. Same guy. The colder they were, the hotter I got. If men were pleasant to be around, interested in what I had to say, loyal, honest, helpful—and if they showed they liked me—I had no use for them. No, I was transfixed by the 007 type—won't commit, good-looking, great body, edgy-dangerous, manly, and focused on anything but me. What made me believe that love was not love without misery? And if I didn't believe that, why did I choose distant men who did not love me, or who eventually did love me, at which point I fell—plunk—out of love with them? We are complex creatures, we humans.

Until now, I had never considered taking the time to put my love life under a microscope. I'd thought of impatience as that itchy feeling you get when you're stuck in line. I was beginning to understand: It's *everywhere.* And we trip over impatience whenever we choose easy answers to the problems that repetitively come up in relationship. After all, why look at what's really behind our pain when we all know it's the *guy's* fault? All those years spent blaming, weeping, and eventually waiting, waiting for the next twitch in my spider's web—when would enough be enough?

D. Growth Practice

- For today, try to find value in the quiet, slow moments of your life. This idea is completely against our cultural norms. Try it anyway. Work to consciously relax into these moments. Maybe use them to get off by yourself for awhile. Try to find some time to spend in Nature—in a park or by water somewhere. If you get antsy, look for a "should," its related fear, and your reality.

AFTERNOON

E. Thinking/Journaling

Choose one of the following:

- Think back on your relationships. Can you find unhealthy similarities among your ex-partners? What about your current partner, if you have one? Is there a recognizable pain around these relationships? How have they ended? Why? Try not to blame the other person or yourself for what happened. Try to identify the lessons that were there for each of you to learn. Ask yourself what you learned—lessons that you carried with you. If those lessons are rooted in anger, look for your "should," your fear, and your reality. You may wish to write about this in your journal.

- When you get a little down, how do you use that time? Do you automatically distract yourself with food or something else? Do you let your mood just drag you down? Could you use it to ask yourself what's actually going on with you?

EVENING

F. Consciousness Expansion

- Try to identify at least one way in which impatience harms your relationships. Could you start to release impatience in the interest of deepening those relationships?

G. Think About

It's not easy to root out the habit of shifting responsibility, of pointing fingers. For years, I avoided taking responsibility whenever I could. Everything was always someone else's fault.

We know why an accident happens when we allow ourselves to get distracted and can't avoid an oncoming car. But we can't always discover why things happen as they do. At such times, maybe the only thing we have any control over is our response. What kinds of responses are possible when we're in pain? When we're angry? Consider letting *"What can I learn from this?"* be your guide.

√ *Look back. What was the change in yourself that you were considering making a few days ago? How is that going?*

Good Night Meditation

Relax completely for a few minutes in silence, eyes closed. Ask yourself: What did I learn today? What did I share with another? What could I have improved on? How can I bring myself into better alignment with my soul mind?

Patience: Day 10

MORNING
Complete A, B, C, and D.

A. Meditation

1. *Invitation*

- Rub your palms together briskly for a few seconds.

- Then, rest your hands, palms up, in your lap or on your thighs.

- Make a circle with thumb and forefinger with the remaining fingers relaxed.

- Sit quietly for a few moments, eyes closed.

- With eyes still closed, raise them to focus on an imaginary small dot in the middle of your forehead. Maintain that focus throughout the meditation. Hold a receptive attitude.

2. *This Day's Intention*

- When you are ready to shift into making your intention, think to yourself:
  I will release the desire to speed things up.

- Repeat that thought:
  I will release the desire to speed things up.

3. *Releasing and Relaxing*

- After a few moments, release your intention and rest in peaceful, receptive inner connection for a few minutes. Release any thoughts that come up and return to your meditation.

4. *Return*

- When you are ready, take a couple of deep breaths, open your eyes, and bring yourself to full consciousness of where you are.

5. *Start the Day*

- With eyes open, say aloud:
  I will release the desire to speed things up.

B. Quotation

> When you see a growing plant, you don't pull it up by the roots to find out how healthy it is. It's enough to see that it has broken through the ground.
>
> —The Lecturer

C. Life Story: *Breath of Life*

In my early teens, I could not wait for tomorrow—which I was certain had to be better than today. Makeup helped me look older from the neck up, but nothing could hide the fact that my body was flat—everywhere. Childhood was so dull. You couldn't do anything without someone's permission. Real women had freedom. Real women had a superstructure. Real women had *breasts*.

I headed for the lingerie department at a large store in Los Angeles. Aisles of bras in all colors were dizzying in number. How did any woman figure out what size she was? Fingering lacy bras, I pretended to shop. I was looking for clues. Women would wander around a bit, make a choice, pay, and leave. No one else seemed confused about the process.

My attention was drawn to a teenaged girl who was being steered by her large, well-dressed mother toward a saleswoman. The mother spoke to the saleswoman—who reached inside the girl's coat to grab her breasts! The girl blushed. I was in shock. No one had ever touched me that intimately—and no stranger was going to start now! I chose a pretty underwire style, a 38C in white, and paid for it. I was still just a skinny, long-legged colt—probably no more than 32" around. What was the difference between an "A" cup and a "D" cup? I couldn't ask. Some snaky-fingered saleswoman would feel the goods if I did. I wanted big, and 38C sounded *big*.

When I tried on the bra at home, my little soft-boiled eggs were lost in grapefruit-sized cups that wrinkled and sagged. The bra itself swam loosely around my body unless I took a deep breath—and held it—to make the most of what I didn't have.

The first time I wore that bra was in a school carpool with three female classmates. With shoulders thrown back and self-satisfied smile gleaming, I proudly announced I now "had to" wear a 38C bra. One girl looked surprised. *"You must have a really big back!"* It wasn't the admiring response I expected.

I kept filling my lungs all day to hold my bra more or less in place, which made talking difficult.

Each morning, I stood before a mirror, hoping that by staring sourly at what I had—and visualizing what I wanted—I could hurry Nature along. I wanted to fill my bra and breathe, too! Visualization didn't work. Neither did bust-building exercises. I continued to believe that there were secrets out there—creams and ointments—that could make breasts grow overnight. All fiction.

I was 16 when my body finally caught up with my mind and filled my bra, which was right about on schedule—Nature's schedule, not mine.

D. Growth Practice

- For today, concentrate on allowing everything to proceed at its own pace, rather than wishing for the weekend to come sooner, for a call to come sooner, or for a computer to give you that information *now*, not ten seconds from now. Whenever you feel impatient, relax and focus on something around you that you would otherwise never notice. Be there in your moment.

AFTERNOON

E. Thinking/Journaling

- Can you recall a time in life when you wanted something to hurry up and happen? Write down the details. How do you feel about that period in your life now? Explain.

EVENING

F. Consciousness Expansion

- Mentally review the day's events. How well were you able to exercise patience when faced with a potentially anxious moment, a moment when you ordinarily would have felt irritated at how slowly the world moves when you want it to speed up?

- The next time you watch a movie or a television drama, try to identify when characters are being moved by soul mind, and when they are moved by outer mind.

G. Think About

I've tried to bend reality to fit my wishes since I can remember. I recall a lot of wishing and not a lot of positive results. Nothing was ever good enough just as it was. The day wasn't sunny enough. The traffic was too heavy to suit me. Some guy didn't call when he said he would. My hips were too broad, my hair too curly. Life in general was out of sync. Does any of this sound familiar? Will you try living one entire day during which you are pleased—even grateful—for everything that comes your way? I'm not talking smiley-faced grateful—just being appreciative and looking for what's in the moment.

Good Night Meditation

Relax completely for a few minutes in silence, eyes closed. Ask yourself what you learned this day, what you shared with another, what you could have done better, and how you can bring yourself into better alignment with your soul mind.

Patience: Day 11

MORNING
Please do A, B, C, and D.

A. Meditation

1. *Invitation*

- Rub your palms together briskly for a few seconds.

- Then, rest your hands, palms up, in your lap or on your thighs.

- Make a circle with thumb and forefinger with the remaining fingers relaxed.

- Sit quietly for a few moments, eyes closed.

- With eyes still closed, raise them to focus on an imaginary small dot in the middle of your forehead. Maintain that focus throughout the meditation. Hold a receptive attitude.

2. *This Day's Intention*

- When you are ready to shift into making your intention, think to yourself:
  I will stay alert and conscious of safety.

- Repeat that thought:
  I will stay alert and conscious of safety.

3. *Releasing and Relaxing*

- After a few moments, release your intention and rest in peaceful, receptive inner connection for a few minutes. Release any thoughts that come up and return to your meditation.

4. *Return*

- When you are ready, take a couple of deep breaths, open your eyes, and bring yourself to full consciousness of where you are.

5. *Start the Day*

- With eyes open, say aloud:
  I will stay alert and conscious of safety.

B. Quotation

> Patience calls for an alert mind—absentmindedness will get you into trouble. Pay attention to what's going on around you. Too many people have been killed because they did not keep an eye on traffic. They died with their minds on something that seemed more important at the time.
>
> —The Lecturer

C. Life Story: *Bungee Jumper*

I sometimes think about the young bungee jumper whose story I heard on public radio. I picture her as trim, in jeans, and with her long hair pulled back into a sassy ponytail. She wears a heavy sweatshirt to protect her arms from rope burns during that breathless fall.

She jumps. You can almost hear the bungee cord sizzle and whip through the empty air —punctuated suddenly by her strangled cry of pain. She is hanging hundreds of feet above a canyon floor by her ponytail—now badly tangled in the bungee cord. The girl rummages roughly, blindly through her pack for a knife. Whipping the blade up and back, it takes just two quick slices to sever the ponytail. And the bungee cord, as well.

I've always wondered if I would have had more presence of mind, more patience under the circumstances. I like to think I would have reached up and hung from the rope by my arms, not my hair, while hollering, *"Help! Hey! Pull me up—now!!"*

D. Growth Practice

- For today, focus on consciously keeping yourself healthy and whole, no matter how much you want to go on autopilot as you drive or cross a street. When your mind wanders, bring it home. Choose a pleasant place for a walk—or if the place isn't especially pleasant in itself, use your mind to make it so.

AFTERNOON

E. Thinking/Journaling

- Do you tend to get frustrated when things go wrong—when you hit too many red lights, or you run out of money before payday? Write about a time that you can remember one such situation, how you reacted to it, and how you would like to respond to similar situations in a more conscious manner. Can you find a "should" here? What's the fear? The reality?

EVENING

F. Consciousness Expansion

- Spend a little time in gratitude for making it safely through this day.

G. Think About

I've almost caused traffic accidents in the past because my body was moving through space while my brain was on walkabout. Why do we forget the lessons buried in these near-disasters? Maybe it's because our outer mind usually returns just in time to avoid trouble. Outer mind says, *"Hey, nothing happened. What's the big deal? Forget it!"* And we do. Keep your eyes open for absentminded moments, no matter how small. Try to be increasingly conscious of what's going on around you—and inside you.

Good Night Meditation

Relax completely for a few minutes in silence, eyes closed. Ask yourself what you learned this day, what you shared with another, what you could have done better, and how you can bring yourself into greater alignment with your soul mind.

Patience: Day 12

MORNING
Please do A, B, C, and D.

A. Meditation

1. *Invitation*

- Rub your palms together briskly for a few seconds.
- Then, rest your hands, palms up, in your lap or on your thighs.
- Make a circle with thumb and forefinger with the remaining fingers relaxed.
- Sit quietly for a few moments, eyes closed.
- With eyes still closed, raise them to focus on an imaginary small dot in the middle of your forehead. Maintain that focus throughout the meditation. Hold a receptive attitude.

2. *This Day's Intention*

- When you are ready to shift into making your intention, think to yourself:
  I will use my time well.
- Repeat that thought:
  I will use my time well.

3. *Releasing and Relaxing*

- After a few moments, release your intention and rest in peaceful, receptive inner connection for a few minutes. Release any thoughts that come up and return to your meditation.

4. *Return*

- When you are ready, take a couple of deep breaths, open your eyes, and bring yourself to full consciousness of where you are.

5. *Start the Day*

- With eyes open, say aloud:
  I will use my time well.

B. Quotation

> Your time here is very short. At the longest, it's very short. Use it well. Be up and doing. Learn from those around you.
>
> —The Lecturer

C. Life Story: *Drums*

Torn between wanting a job I could love and keeping the one I had, I drowned out the pain by filling nights and weekends with Smithsonian Associates' programs. I reveled in Russian chamber music, learned how brains work, and applauded live re-creations of radio plays from the 40s.

One warm spring evening, I went to a concert by Japanese *taiko* drummers. Seven drums sat onstage—two huge ones close to the audience and five smaller drums behind, all cradled by sturdy-looking wooden stands. The drum skins on the big ones were dark brown—with blue-black, tattoo-like designs at their centers. I sat halfway between the big drums—and in the front row. The audience buzzed with anticipation.

Dressed in navy and white cotton folk costumes, sweatbands around their temples, two young women and five men bounded onstage, barefoot. Soon, rhythmic booms and clacks resounded throughout the auditorium, rattling my clavicles. I grinned in delight.

In *taiko*, the energy and life of the moment is everything. Drummers and audience are carried on waves of driving sound. That night, the drummers broke at least five drumsticks apiece with the passion *taiko* calls for. All evening, failed drumsticks split and shot jagged wooden fragments onto the stage or into the audience—which roared its approval. One such fragment clattered to rest near my right foot. I snatched it up.

Standing at the front of the stage, the two women beat exuberantly on the largest drums, their arms flashing, their hair shimmering. One was Japanese, the other a ponytailed blonde American. Bewitched by a performance in Tokyo, the blonde had begged the troupe to teach her their craft. They must have seen the blazing light in her that it takes to be a *taiko* drummer because they made her one of the family—after she passed a few small tests.

At the end of the concert, the women dangled their legs over the edge of the stage and chatted with the audience. The American confided that her first year with the troupe was difficult. She had to patiently clean their practice area "just so" and make tea—lots of tea—for anyone who wanted it. She had to make sure all the drums were cleaned and conditioned properly. And the drumsticks! Enough drumsticks had to be on hand for every practice and every performance. In other words, her training began with the need to submerge her ego/outer mind enough to be an effective member of a Japanese group, rather than a hotshot pretty blonde American girl star. Patience was central to "outer mind training." It was only after she did everything she was asked, did it well, and without the slightest complaint, that her *taiko* drum training began.

I didn't realize that night that the *taiko* troupe had taught me to live again with passion, to do something that engages heart, mind, and soul—to use my time well. The American drummer also taught me about the value of patience as part of an overall goal. The night washed through me, gradually shifting my center of gravity.

Within a few months, I was working one day a week with the Smithsonian Associates. I went on flex time at my day job, putting in ten hours a day four days a week. At the Smithsonian, I spent every Wednesday for a year creating and coordinating programs for the public. Then, it was time to move on. I was no longer willing to aim low, keep my head down, come alive only after work, and plod through the years until retirement. I would look for a job where it was possible to fail—or succeed.

I still have that jaunty piece of drumstick, its autograph pale with the passage of time. It's jammed into the thick knot of a hemp rope in my office—still challenging me to live with passion. Still doing its job.

D. Growth Practice

- Are you living with a sense of passion, doing something that engages your heart, mind, and soul? What turns your light on? If you haven't felt that light lately, what might you do to rediscover it?

AFTERNOON

E. Thinking/Journaling

- When have you felt the most alive in your life and why? Write about the experience, the person/people involved. What value does that experience have for you now?

EVENING

F. Consciousness Expansion

- In what way might a little outer mind training benefit your life? Where might you want to apply it?

G. Think About

It's so easy to slip into complacency, to get comfortable and lazy, to sit back and go on autopilot instead of looking for the challenges, learning as much as we can, giving what we have to give, and discovering our own "blazing light." What would you do with your life if you could? Even if you couldn't make a living at what you love, is there any way you could bring that passion into the life you live?

√ *Look back. How did your day of appreciation go?*

Good Night Meditation

Relax completely for a few minutes in silence, eyes closed. Ask yourself what you learned this day, what you shared with another, what you could have done better, and how you can bring yourself into greater alignment with your soul mind.

Patience: Day 13

MORNING
Work with A, B, C, and D.

A. Meditation

1. *Invitation*

- Rub your palms together briskly for a few seconds.

- Then, rest your hands, palms up, in your lap or on your thighs.

- Make a circle with thumb and forefinger with the remaining fingers relaxed.

- Sit quietly for a few moments, eyes closed.

- With eyes still closed, raise them to focus on an imaginary small dot in the middle of your forehead. Maintain that focus throughout the meditation. Hold a receptive attitude.

2. *This Day's Intention*

- When you are ready to shift into making your intention, think to yourself:
  When I run out of time, I will be patient.

- Repeat:
  When I run out of time, I will be patient.

3. *Releasing and Relaxing*

- After a few moments, release your intention and rest in peaceful, receptive inner connection for a few minutes. Release any thoughts that come up and return to your meditation.

4. *Return*

- When you are ready, take a couple of deep breaths, open your eyes, and bring yourself to full consciousness of where you are.

5. *Start the Day*

- With eyes open, say aloud:
  When I run out of time, I will be patient.

B. Quotation

> We never seem to have enough time to do what we would like to do. That is an opportunity to apply patience. We often find that the outer mind encourages impatience, instead.
>
> —The Lecturer

C. Life Story: *Chasing Time*

At the office, I had an edgy desire for people to cut to the chase. My tightly wound energy telegraphed, *"Don't waste my time."* I never made personal calls and only talked business when I was on the clock. After several years of lackluster jobs, I had finally found a position that was deeply involving and satisfying. So, I *worked*. Home was only a place to sleep and recharge my batteries for the next day. Weekends often found me at the office. My mind was always on business. I expected the same from my staff and was irritated when I found them chit-chatting in the kitchen for more than five minutes. While I heated water for tea, my scowl would dampen their conversation and send them quickly back to their desks.

One fairly new staff member began stopping by my office most mornings to talk—and not about work, either. From behind my large desk, which was covered—stacked—with papers and books, I'd see Anna coming and feel my blood pressure slowly rise. There she was, in my office, sitting down, ready to chat away another few minutes of my precious work day!

I was torn. A part of me was irritated by the interruptions. Another part responded to her patient, friendly overtures. Despite myself, I began to look forward to her visits. I was a loner by nature, but Anna faithfully built those minutes into our day—while I kept fighting the urge to check my e-mails.

Over a period of months, we spoke of our fears and hardships, our frustrations and our dreams. We talked politics, hers and mine. We shared stories of her home life and the roller-coaster ride that characterized my relationships. In the process, we wove between us threads of commonality and differences, respect, and discovery—the warm bonds people loop through one another's lives while building a deep and lasting friendship.

When I left that job, I realized how much I valued those few moments that had begun my work day, that made me recall who we both were as members of a great family that does not, cannot, live by work alone—no matter what the culture tells us. The question wasn't whether I was working hard enough and long enough. I was. I always got the job done and done well. So did Anna. The question was whether I could find the patience to act human in the midst of it all—whether I laughed, connected, and could accept others and myself for what we were—for *all* of what we were. If I could do that, at the end of my days, I would not have to ask, *"Is that all there is?"*

D. Growth Practice

- Try not to be obsessive about checking e-mail—maybe take a holiday from it. Once a week, perhaps? Scary thought? What's the "should" here? The fear? The reality?

AFTERNOON

E. Thinking/Journaling
Choose one of the following:

- Write a journal page about your relationship with time. Is it a healthy relationship, or not? If you feel driven by time, how could you change that? Would you like to?

- What do you do to make sure that you spend real time (not just electronic time) with the special people in your life? Do you believe that friends and/or family get enough of your time? If not, what could you do about that?

EVENING

F. Consciousness Expansion

- If you feel chained to time, trapped by time, burdened by time, chased by time, consider making dates with yourself (in ink) on your calendar to do things you do not usually permit yourself to do because you're too busy running. Make sure your dates with yourself are not the first ones you break under pressure. Cherish them as you would cherish dates made with your closest friend. When you think about it, isn't that what you should be to yourself? Aren't you the only person that you know for sure will be with you to your very last breath?

G. Think About

If you are always watching the clock, try spending a day without time. Do not set an alarm. Sleep in (you're probably sleep-deprived anyway—consider it a gift to yourself.) Cover the face of your clock-radio. Do not wear your watch. Cover over all references to time in your house. Be obsessive about it this once. If you use the computer, tape over the little clock portion—do whatever you can to discover how time spirals out with Nature when left to itself, instead of being trapped into small, constantly measured mechanical increments. Eat when you're hungry, not by the clock.

Go to bed when you're tired, not when the clock says you should. If you live with someone, try to get that person to take a little time vacation with you—otherwise, take it by yourself. As amazing as it may sound, not every moment has to be packed with activities or TV. Realize that the better part of who you are is unconcerned with time. That part of you does not drive you to miss so much of the richness of life while packing endless activities into every corner of every day. Sit back. Take a deep breath. Smile to yourself. Relax.

Good Night Meditation

Relax completely for a few minutes in silence, eyes closed. Ask yourself what you learned this day, what you shared with another, what you could have done better, and how you can bring yourself into greater alignment with your soul mind.

Patience: Day 14

MORNING
Do A, B, C, and D.

A. Meditation

1. *Invitation*

- Rub your palms together briskly for a few seconds.

- Then, rest your hands, palms up, in your lap or on your thighs.

- Make a circle with thumb and forefinger with the remaining fingers relaxed.

- Sit quietly for a few moments, eyes closed.

- With eyes still closed, raise them to focus on an imaginary small dot in the middle of your forehead. Maintain that focus throughout the meditation. Hold a receptive attitude.

2. *This Day's Intention*

- When you are ready to shift into making your intention, think to yourself:
  I will focus on the moment.

- Repeat that thought:
  I will focus on the moment.

3. *Releasing and Relaxing*

- After a few moments, release your intention and rest in peaceful, receptive inner connection for a few minutes. Release any thoughts that come up and return to your meditation.

4. *Return*

- When you are ready, take a couple of deep breaths, open your eyes, and bring yourself to full consciousness of where you are.

5. *Start the Day*

- With eyes open, say aloud:
  I will focus on the moment.

B. Quotation

> Patience calls for keeping your focus on the moment. Here is where you are. Earth School is in session when other human beings provide us with a wealth of confusing and difficult opportunities to interact with unlovely parts of ourselves. That's their job. They perform it to perfection.
>
> —The Lecturer

C. Life Story: *What's in Front*

After more failed relationships than I could count, I was as unhappy as I had ever been. The romance that was supposed to turn my life around was in shreds.

In the house that Sunday, nothing could compete with my internal drama. I hadn't eaten breakfast or lunch. I was still padding around in my nightgown at noon, crying. Nothing mattered but the pain.

My brain was *smoking*. If I could solve complex professional problems, which I did every weekday, I could surely solve this one. It was just a matter of making him understand, of getting him to say, *"You're right, of course! I can't wait to meet all your needs, which are far more important than mine—not that you know or care what my needs are. Take the clay of my personality and mold it. I am yours to command."* My thoughts weren't that specific. You get the idea.

Will took pride in being one of those men who cannot be domesticated. I was discovering that although he is capable of loving deeply, he refuses the leash. I had been certain that all I had to do was convince him. Teach him. *Tweak* him.

Tears still sliding down my cheeks, I flipped the light switch in the walk-in closet. The bulb popped loudly, flashed, and died. Something *else* gone wrong! Sighing loudly, I went off to scramble through the kitchen pantry, looking for one functioning bulb.

That morning, I had said a little generalized prayer for help with my "problem." No answer. No thunderbolt of a solution split the sky.

It was now late afternoon. I had two light bulbs in my hands. One was good. The other wasn't. Suddenly, a sentence arrived fully formed in my mind: *"Deal with what's in front of you."*

Deal with what's in front of me? I looked down at the bulbs, then up at the empty light socket. Putting aside the bad bulb, I stepped up onto my footstool and screwed the good one in. And there was light!

I spent the rest of that day observing and responding to my life as it unrolled before me, moment by moment. Every time my brain veered into past painful memories, or into my fantasies of a future with Will (who was clearly *not* in front of me so I could hardly deal with *him*), I stopped. Focusing on what was there, I dealt with it. Time after time.

The tears left. The drama that had taken up every square inch of my life slid slowly offstage like smoke.

My ever-active outer mind had formed an intoxicating image of what Will had to be and do for my happiness. Part of me knew it would never happen. Pain was the payoff, not love. I was dancing with a shadowy, unlovely, outer mind-based part of myself. I could not even see Will as separate from me. Did he, could he, have needs and wishes of his own? Might he even have the right to pursue his happiness in any form he chose? As that thought filtered through my mind, another thought soon followed it: If he had that right, maybe I did, too. And maybe, while walking our respective paths, we could meet in the middle and learn how to share—love. Astounding thought!

D. Growth Practice

- For today, consciously focus on what's in front of you, no matter what the distractions are—internal or external. Look for a way to spend some time with yourself in Nature.

AFTERNOON

E. Thinking/Journaling

- Can you see growth in your personal journey, a journey that for most of us begins with an unswerving focus on ourselves, our wants, our needs, our concerns? Write about this journey. Include any "detours" that show a growing concern and interest in family, friends, community, and the larger global picture. Do you have goals larger than personal goals? What are they? What's your timeframe to achieve them? Is something holding you back? What could that be? How could you overcome it?

EVENING

F. Consciousness Expansion

- When was the last time someone gave you an opportunity to interact with an unlovely part of yourself? What happened? What did you learn?

- Someone has said that if we love other people (and not just ourselves, which is when we use others just to get our needs met), we want what's best for them—their own highest good. In a few words, write in your journal what you believe to be your own highest good. Who in your life contributes (or has contributed) to your learning, your growth, and your expansion of consciousness? What have you learned by this person's (or these people's) example? Is there anything you do that does not contribute to your highest good? What might that be?

G. Think About

What do you most want from others? Is it love? Is it respect? Is it honesty? Whatever you most want to receive from others, will you try giving it to yourself?

> √ *Look back. How are you doing with bringing a sense of patience to your mind when you feel pulled in all directions by stress?*

Good Night Meditation

Relax completely for a few minutes in silence, eyes closed. Ask yourself what you learned this day, what you shared with another, what you could have done better, and how you can bring yourself into greater alignment with your soul mind.

Chapter Eleven
Workbook: On Perseverance

*I*t takes nerve for the person who has lived my life to recommend perseverance. I've paid the rent by hopscotching through jobs as an English conversation teacher, TV newscaster, talk show host, hospital staff writer, production coordinator, multi-marketer of therapeutic magnets (an experience that ate up my savings and taught me the value of a dollar), part-time program coordinator for the Smithsonian's Resident Associates program, editorial assistant, secretary, and waitress (for only two weeks—I couldn't remember people's orders)—among other things. Through the years, some job interviewers found my checkered background fascinating. Others couldn't sweep me out the door fast enough, *"My God,"* they must have thought, *"What next? Dog catcher? Astronaut?"*

Did you ever see that old Japanese movie where the samurai kicks one tattered sandal high up into the air at a fork in the road? Spinning end over end, the sandal lands—and the samurai slouches off along the road his sandal chooses. At many of my forks in the road, I used about that level of penetrating research to make important decisions.

I also made a habit of not sticking with relationships past the rocky phase. When the going got rough, I got gone.

This book almost didn't get written. I would either put in obsessive 14-hour days or I'd abandon it—for weeks. In 2006, at a year-end retreat with Neale Donald Walsch, author of the *Conversations with God* books, I asked for advice. Neale said, *"Promise yourself you will spend an hour every day writing your book. You will be amazed at how much you can get done that way."* Those words wrapped my life around the project and gave the book a heartbeat.

For the past 12 years, I have been with the same job—still learning and still enjoying it. And for the past six years, I have been with the same man—with no desire to go trolling. It's not that I made up my mind to stick with a job or a man no matter what. In the job department, it has to do with knowing what I like and am good at—and choosing that. In the man department, I chose someone with a quirky sense of humor, a mellow nature, a kind heart, and a keen mind. We share much that could only be called spiritual. I had started going after the type of work and the kind of man that fit the person I wanted to be—rather than grabbing at the wind and hoping for the best. I'm no longer running around, looking everywhere for someone or something to save or complete me. Charity, they say, begins at home. So does inner peace.

The lecturer rarely spoke of perseverance all by itself. It was usually "patience *and* perseverance." In order to practice perseverance, I had to be willing to patiently put my whims on a back burner to pursue worthwhile goals over time. If I didn't, I lost focus and the whims won out. For years, perseverance had just occupied space in the box marked, *Stuff I Really Should Look at—Someday.*

Please make patience your walking stick as we climb Mt. Perseverance.

Perseverance: Day 15

MORNING
Please do A, B, C, and D.

A. Meditation

1. *Invitation*

   • Rub your palms together briskly for a few seconds.

   • Then, rest your hands, palms up, in your lap or on your thighs.

   • Make a circle with thumb and forefinger with the remaining fingers relaxed.

   • Sit quietly for a few moments, eyes closed.

   • With eyes still closed, raise them to focus on an imaginary small dot in the middle of your forehead. Maintain that focus for seven or eight minutes. Hold a receptive attitude.

2. *This Day's Intention*

   • When you are ready to shift into making your intention, think to yourself:
   I will set aside fantasy and embrace reality.

   • Repeat that thought:
   I will set aside fantasy and embrace reality.

3. *Releasing and Relaxing*

   • After a few moments, release your intention and rest in peaceful, receptive inner connection for a few minutes. Release any thoughts that come up and return to your meditation.

4. *Return*

   • When you are ready, take a couple of deep breaths, open your eyes, and bring yourself to full consciousness of where you are.

5. *Start the Day*

   • With eyes open, say aloud:
   I will set aside fantasy and embrace reality.

B. Quotation

> Fantasies may seem attractive—especially compared to our reality. In the end, they do not serve us well. They blind us to truth. They keep us pursuing shadows. Our paths require light, not darkness.
>
> —The Lecturer

C. Life Story: *Fantasy Father*

My father never wanted children. But when my mother became pregnant, he dreamed of a son. So great was his disappointment in my gender that he had a vasectomy days after my birth.

My father kept his distance, withholding everything healthy fathers give their daughters—unconditional love, support, and respect. And when he drank, his resentment toward the woman who had brought me into the world—and me—erupted. Finally, when I was five, my mother and I ran away from the alcoholic rants, the punches, the black eyes.

This is by way of explaining a fantasy I steadfastly maintained about my father, one that had no basis whatsoever in reality. I knew the reasons we had run away. But more important than the man himself was the fantasy I created around him. In my mind, he *had* to return. And when he returned, he would regret not being a part of my life. He would love me. And I would be free of the suspicion that he had abandoned the only child he would ever have because she was not good enough.

After the divorce, he visited once—when I was eight. He then wrote my mother, saying he would not return until I was "of an age of understanding." Clinging to those words, I tried to become what I thought of as perfect—or at least better. I tried to figure out what the "age of understanding" meant, and I finally settled on my 18th birthday. During the last uneventful days of my 17th year, I felt excited, whole, and at peace.

The morning I turned 18, I woke up early. Pulling my clothes on, I half-ran to the front of the house and peered out the window, looking for his car. My heart was pounding, but the street was empty. So I headed for my classes at Los Angeles City College. He would turn up—maybe take me to lunch. He didn't. After school, I hurried home. He wasn't there, either. Oh, of course not. Obviously, he wanted to share dinner with me. I rushed through my homework and waited, anxious and happy.

My mother couldn't understand why I picked at my food that evening.

I hadn't told her that I was going to eat with my father, to laugh with him and show him what he had missed all those years. It would be a surprise.

As the hours ticked by, I wondered why he was so late. Finally, I understood—18 is not the age of understanding. You have to be 21! I felt such a fool. And I put myself through the same build-up and let-down for my 21st birthday. When he also didn't show up.

Something inside me believed I needed my father's validation before I could become a woman. I didn't get that validation. For years, I swung back and forth between anger and telling myself I didn't care if I never saw him again. Once, I pictured him in the throes of a terrible illness that I could have helped him survive—if only he'd found me in time.

My fantasy image inflated him beyond a living, breathing human being. I didn't allow myself to work through my grief process because I refused to believe that I had lost him. I had only misplaced him. And the man I had misplaced was both a dark, disapproving judge and a savior who held the key to a daughter's life. He was Pain and Love in one—I truly did not know that love for a man could exist apart from pain. And I did not stop resenting my father for holding out on me until I started learning how to love and accept myself—my real self, not my "perfect" self—and doing it without his approval.

Will calls my father a "sperm donor." It's accurate. Without that one sperm, I would not have life, so I'm grateful for it. I'm also grateful that we left him. As much as the fantasy fallout scarred my relationships with men, the reality of his daily resentment and disapproval—not to mention the beatings—would have been worse. I have told only three people—until now—about how many years I was ruled by that fantasy. It was a skewed vision of love created by my outer mind, fueled by fears and doubts.

The image of my father was blurred. It took years to put together pieces of the few stories that my mother told me about him. When I did, I saw an angry, jealous little boy whose father beat him, a boy whose sister was his father's favorite. To my father, love was quantitative—there was only so much to go around. How could he give me love when he had received so little? My mother, too, had been raised to believe that love was a kind of human currency. You shared it when people deserved it. You cut it off when they didn't. I knew what it was to give people I loved "the silent treatment" when my feelings were hurt.

My mother and father married two weeks after they met. Theirs was a passionate union. At last, my father believed, he had a love all his own. I was a constant reminder of his loss. *"Ain't I enough for you?"* he asked my mother once when she insisted on nursing me instead of making love with him. Down deep, he feared that she loved me best. He was ultimately proven right.

Perseverance had nothing to do with my focus on my father. Perseverance after a college education, for example, leads to greater understanding and growth. What I pursued so relentlessly was only a fantasy that kept me tethered to a heavy post. I walked around and around that post, asking questions that had no answers. *"Why doesn't he love me? What did I do wrong? When will he come back? How can I please him?"* I could only have pleased him by being born male—better yet, by not being born at all. And that I could not change.

D. Growth Practice

- Today, think about your father, your mother, or the person who was most responsible for your care as you grew up. What was your childhood like? What do you see as positive? Negative? Can you see any similarities between those who raised you and the people you are attracted to now? If you can, how does that make you feel? What's the strongest "should" you can remember from your early days? The fear? The reality?

AFTERNOON

E. Thinking/Journaling

- If your relationship with a family member changed through the years, describe what has taken place. What did you hope for? What did you get? What did you give? Have you ever felt disappointed by the gulf between your fantasies and the reality around family?

EVENING

F. Consciousness Expansion

- Many of us walk through life always circling back, trying to fix the past. For example, those who had distant fathers may think they want affectionate mates, but be attracted to loners. A man whose mother had psychological problems may be attracted to troubled women. Life always gives us second chances. If we view those opportunities with the same dependence on having someone else fill all the holes in our hearts, we will be disappointed. It is only when we grow beyond what was considered "normal" in our own childhoods that we can make peace with the past. Then, we can start to connect with others in a mutually supportive and loving way, not just grasp at them to meet our needs. How much of your life has been spent in circling back to fix the past? If you have that pattern in life, do you want to change it? How might you go about that?

G. Think About

A recurring theme in my life has been the powerful desire to get other people to meet my needs. I resented that they refused to do as I wished. I told myself that they didn't know any better, so I should forgive them (even though I didn't want to). That gave me no comfort. That's because I was acting like I knew what they would do if they weren't so ignorant. In deciding how others should live their lives, I was giving in to the voice of my outer mind, and the outer mind's song cannot heal a heart in pain.

I only began to feel comforted when I saw that I was focusing on changing the wrong person. Whatever damage was done to me by others was mine to work through, mine to forgive. The other person's acts and words were theirs to work through—their karma. Resenting people for what they had done to me only made me miserable. It did not change what had happened. It did not punish them. It only punished me for not forgiving, and moving on. What about you? Does any of this remind you of yourself?

Good Night Meditation

Relax completely for a few minutes in silence, eyes closed. Ask yourself what you learned this day, what you shared with another, what you could have done better, and how you can bring yourself into greater alignment with your soul mind.

Perseverance: Day 16

MORNING
Please do A, B, C, and D.

A. Meditation

1. *Invitation*

- Rub your palms together briskly for a few seconds.

- Then, rest your hands, palms up, in your lap or on your thighs.

- Make a circle with thumb and forefinger with the remaining fingers relaxed.

- Sit quietly for a few moments, eyes closed.

- With eyes still closed, raise them to focus on an imaginary small dot in the middle of your forehead. Maintain that focus for seven or eight minutes. Hold a receptive attitude.

2. *This Day's Intention*

- When you are ready to shift into making your intention, think to yourself:
  I will consistently pursue my goals.

- Repeat:
  I will consistently pursue my goals.

3. *Releasing and Relaxing*

- After a few moments, release your intention and rest in peaceful, receptive inner connection for a few minutes. Release any thoughts that come up and return to your meditation.

4. *Return*

- When you are ready, take a couple of deep breaths, open your eyes, and bring yourself to full consciousness of where you are.

5. *Start the Day*

- With eyes open, say aloud:
  I will consistently pursue my goals.

B. Quotation

> Be consistent toward your goals, no matter what your outer mind says to you, no matter how hard it tries to mislead you and to deny and deprive you by playing on your fears and your doubts. It is only human to be inconsistent, it seems, but draw yourself back in line. Only through consistency can we accomplish what we want to accomplish.
>
> —The Lecturer

C. Life Story: *The Break*

Frustrated by how long it was taking to get into television news in America, I made an appointment with one of my U.S.C. professors. *"I see talented students in this department,"* I told him, *"but they aren't getting on-camera jobs. What's the secret?"* *"Take classes,"* he said. *"Work hard. Be lucky."* With that, he stood up. I didn't. I'd had enough of the canned answer. I wanted the *real* one.

We stared at each other. Finally, he said, *"Take Nate Kaplan's broadcast writing class. He's a news consultant for several TV stations. If he likes you, he'll find you a job."* The bad part was that Nate Kaplan limited his classes to 12 students—and the semester would start in only three weeks. I ran down to the Registrar's office. Not only was the roster full, but four additional names were wait-listed.

All of my life, I have given up too easily in the face of obstacles. In this case, my outer mind played on my doubts and fears, saying, *"You're not ready. You need to take many more classes."* Something made me ignore that voice and put my name down on the wait-list as #5. Maybe I could audit the class.

I arrived ten minutes early, sat in the back of the room, and spread my books, jacket, lunch, and papers in a circle around me. I wanted to look like I was in that class to *stay*, like it would take a small bomb or at least the school's entire football team to dislodge me.

Nate was short, in his early 60s, balding, with a little paunch. Sweat glistened on his upper lip. Speaking in public was clearly not his favorite activity. I liked his willingness to exceed his comfort level in order to share what he knew. Little good it would do me, but I liked Nate Kaplan.

He called out the names of those who were registered. Eleven students responded. The twelfth one did not. Nate then called out the names of the four wait-listed students, one by one. All no-shows. Mine was the 17th name. When he said *"Carol Kline,"* I shot my hand in the air and choked on *"Here!"* Laughing, Nate motioned for me to come take a seat up front.

My life's one goal was to learn what Nate Kaplan had to teach— and to impress him into finding me a job. Every night, I polished my stories. I memorized what Nate taught us about the differences between broadcast English and everyday English, about how to write an exciting lead to a story, about saving something tasty for the last sentence or two. I allowed nothing to distract me.

Six weeks after class started, Nate asked for my demo tape—a video of news stories I had researched, written, edited, and voiced in news production class. My best story was about people who lived in expensive homes up in the canyons around Los Angeles. Every few years, mudslides filled their beautiful pools or cracked their walls and windows. But they always rebuilt on exactly the same spot—and dared Nature to do it again. *"How could we live anywhere else?"* asked one man. *"I mean, just look at all this."* He raised an arm, indicating gorgeous trees, a clear blue sky, and an unlimited panoramic view of the city below. My camera zoomed in on his mud-filled pool while recording what he had to say about the joys of canyon living.

The story itself was solid, but you'd never see it on the 6 o'clock news— and for good reason. It looked like I'd shot it through blue glass. I never did figure out the mechanics of twisting the camera's dials to achieve "white balance," the method the pros use to make sure colors are true.

Nate didn't care about my technical incapabilities. He had a job for me as a reporter in North Carolina if I wanted it. If I *wanted* it! My hands shaking with excitement, I got on the phone for an interview with the news director at tiny WGHP-TV in High Point, North Carolina. Jim Bennett had seen my demo tape. He laughed at my photographic "skills," but he liked me. Without finishing out the semester, I headed for the East Coast with Stu.

The neighborhood was seedy, the hotel—the home of the TV station—looked like a sinking ship. But this was my chance. Six months later, the station's female anchor left and I took her spot. I was one happy woman.

Perseverance got me the job. Keeping it was something else.

D. Growth Practice

- Today, look at how doubt or fear may be keeping you from moving forward with something you want. Is this doubt or fear based on reality, or is the outer mind sabotaging you?

AFTERNOON

E. Thinking/Journaling

- Write about how fear or doubts about yourself kept you from doing something you wanted to do. What were the circumstances? Who was involved? If you had it to do over again, how would you handle it?

EVENING

F. Consciousness Expansion

- Try to think of something you would like to achieve by this date—next year. Are you ready to sketch out a timeline, together with sub-goals that will help you move toward the larger goal? Why is this goal important to you? What are you willing to give up to achieve it? Ink in the dates of the steps you will take to reach this goal on your calendar. The more you can see yourself carrying out your goal, the more powerfully that image will motivate you.

G. Think About

Many of us have ideas and dreams and not a lot of follow-through. Sometimes, the idea for an invention, a widget, may pop into our heads— just like that. The idea is great. We do nothing with it. And we learn later that someone else has come up with the same invention and gotten a patent! We might have sold a million widgets and moved to a gorgeous house in Hawaii—if we hadn't been so lazy. In what other ways do we hold ourselves back by a failure to follow through? Can you think of specific examples in your life?

√ *Look back. Have you been able to consistently focus on what's in front of you?*

Good Night Meditation

Relax completely for a few minutes in silence, eyes closed. Ask yourself what you learned this day, what you shared with another, what you could have done better, and how you can bring yourself into greater alignment with your soul mind.

Perseverance: Day 17

MORNING
Do A, B, C, and D.

A. Meditation

1. *Invitation*

- Rub your palms together briskly for a few seconds.

- Then, rest your hands, palms up, in your lap or on your thighs.

- Make a circle with thumb and forefinger with the remaining fingers relaxed.

- Sit quietly for a few moments, eyes closed.

- With eyes still closed, raise them to focus on an imaginary small dot in the middle of your forehead. Maintain that focus throughout the meditation. Hold a receptive attitude.

2. *This Day's Intention*

- When you are ready to shift into making your intention, think to yourself:
I will learn, grow, and expand in consciousness.

- Repeat that thought:
I will learn, grow, and expand in consciousness.

3. *Releasing and Relaxing*

- After a few moments, release your intention and rest in peaceful, receptive inner connection for a few minutes. Release any thoughts that come up and return to your meditation.

4. *Return*

- When you are ready, take a couple of deep breaths, open your eyes, and bring yourself to full consciousness of where you are.

5. *Start the Day*

- With eyes open, say aloud:
I will learn, grow, and expand in consciousness.

B. Quotation

> Persistence is important. Human beings tend to be indecisive.
> It's only good to vacillate in the younger years as we try
> to decide what we want to be. Persistence will help us make
> the most of our opportunities to learn, grow, and expand in
> consciousness.
>
> —The Lecturer

C. Life Story: *Impossible*

After I'd been fired from WGHP (which is another story for another day), I was hired part time at two North Carolina universities to teach broadcast journalism. My favorite class was broadcast English, which gave me the opportunity to teach people born and raised in North Carolina how to speak the kind of English required to get jobs anywhere outside the South. That first semester, I spent many hours creating ways to help them access the sounds and speech patterns they heard only in movies, on television, or from me.

One early assignment I gave the students was to go home after school and take a hot, relaxing tub bath. They were to talk into a tape recorder about their day or about their dreams for the future. The only requirement was to speak Standard English for five minutes.

At the next class, I played all of their tapes for the class and we critiqued them. Several of the students had been certain they already spoke Standard English—especially one young man from New Jersey. While we listened, the students themselves identified the drawls, the sing-song phrasing, and the muddy diction.

We began every class with warm-ups that reached for resonance, Standard English, and clarity of diction. We were so enthusiastic we got teased by people in nearby classes—including the professors. But my students were making progress!

I was at my best that first semester. By the second semester, my level of engagement was slipping. I vacillated, trying one idea and then another—with no internal unifying force behind my efforts. And by the third semester, I had my bag of tricks that I turned to, just as some other teachers do (not the good ones—good teachers never lose their edge or their excitement). I look back now on that time with nostalgia. I loved teaching, but I lost my enthusiasm when I allowed habit to substitute for creativity. I simply made copies of previous semesters' exercises without any thought for how good they were or whether they were what my current students most needed. Without fresh demands on my creativity, it became just a job. And there was something else, something I did not even realize until I wrote this. I had also gotten caught up in yet another go-nowhere romance. Of all the things I wish I could do over in life, those last three semesters are right at the top.

Still, I'll never forget Doug, a broadcast journalism major at Wake Forest University. He was in the last class I taught before moving to Pennsylvania. His enunciation never wavered—it was invariably deep North Carolinian. Doug frequently made fun of his "mush-mouth" diction. While the other students slowly mastered a style of pronunciation, enunciation, and delivery that they could turn on and off at will, Doug could not be consistent. He sometimes said "myself" or "through," but he always slipped back into "mahseff" and "thoo." Every week, he worked hard to earn D's and F's.

It was the day of the Final. Semester grades in that class depended on what students accomplished on this one day. Nothing really mattered in broadcast English except the degree of change they could master—and take with them. Student after student gave individual news deliveries while I made notes.

It was Doug's turn. He strode to the front of the class, turned slowly toward us, and began. From first word to last, Doug delivered the news in his rich, creamy baritone—in perfect Standard English! We sat open-mouthed—then jumped to our feet. Doug's classmates were stomping the floor and cheering. Doug had stayed up all night, practicing the sounds in his five-minute set piece over and over, recording himself, listening to the results, and matching his sounds phonetically to Standard English—until he could do it all without slipping into those bone-deep habits of speech. I had tried to help him. Nothing worked. Finally, I had given up. Doug never gave up on himself. That was key. It was Doug's single-minded focus that brought about his individual miracle, a logically impossible gold-medal performance.

D. Growth Practice

- Today, dig through some of your habits around how you spend your time or your money and pick one that no longer serves you. What might you do instead? What "should" has kept you locked into that outworn habit?

AFTERNOON

E. Thinking/Journaling

- Have you accomplished something that seemed impossible? If you haven't, what about someone you know? Write about who did what, when, where, how, and why. How do you feel about that accomplishment? How important do you believe persistence was to success?

EVENING

F. Consciousness Expansion

- Throw this into your basket of possibilities: What would you like to do that would be helpful or useful to others—something that may have no connection to your career goals or to what you currently do? What are your obstacles? If one of those obstacles is money, could this goal (or something similar) be accomplished less expensively?

G. Think About

I can remember a period of several years during which I gave up on myself. My life was ruled by past disappointments and the fear of future disappointments. What would you have advised me if you had known me then? Will you take your own advice if you ever need it?

√ *Look back. How are you doing with follow-through?*

Good Night Meditation

Relax completely for a few minutes in silence, eyes closed. Ask yourself what you learned this day, what you shared with another, what you could have done better, and how you can bring yourself into greater alignment with your soul mind.

Perseverance: Day 18

MORNING
Accomplish A, B, C, and D.

A. Meditation

1. *Invitation*

- Rub your palms together briskly for a few seconds.

- Then, rest your hands, palms up, in your lap or on your thighs.

- Make a circle with thumb and forefinger with the remaining fingers relaxed.

- Sit quietly for a few moments, eyes closed.

- With eyes still closed, raise them to focus on an imaginary small dot in the middle of your forehead. Maintain that focus throughout the meditation. Hold a receptive attitude.

2. *This Day's Intention*

- When you are ready to shift into making your intention, think to yourself:
  I will conquer what has conquered me in the past.

- Repeat:
  I will conquer what has conquered me in the past.

3. *Releasing and Relaxing*

- After a few moments, release your intention and rest in peaceful, receptive inner connection for a few minutes. Release any thoughts that come up and return to your meditation.

4. *Return*

- When you are ready, take a couple of deep breaths, open your eyes, and bring yourself to full consciousness of where you are.

5. *Start the Day*

- With eyes open, say aloud:
  I will conquer what has conquered me in the past.

B. Quotation

> To fulfill your mission means to conquer what you need to conquer—the individual lessons that you stumble over every day. Your attitude and your perseverance will pay high dividends in this area.
> —The Lecturer

C. Life Story: *Sleepwalker*

One thing I know: Obsession and perseverance are not the same. When I met Karl in Allentown, Pennsylvania, I was 49—and obsessed with the belief that a woman could not survive in her later years without a man. That's what kept me with him for three long years. This is a story about what love is. And is not.

Karl was no icy loner. In the beginning, that was exciting. Soon, Karl was calling many times every day to find out where I was, who I was with, and what I was doing. At first, I soaked up the attention—no man had ever loved me like that!

In time, his attentiveness became restrictive. He pushed me not to return friends' calls. I stopped horseback riding. *"A waste of money,"* he called it. He was glad my family was small and far away—that made me more dependent on him. My life shrank down to mostly Karl. When he asked me to move in, I did. Safe at last.

Karl had a closet full of women's clothes, which he asked me to wear. He said he didn't want the money he'd spent on them to go to waste. That wasn't the real reason. We met three weeks after his beloved wife's death. The clothes were hers. After we'd had yet another fight about my not wanting to wear the clothes, Karl admitted that he wanted me to "become" Gretchen by dressing like her—so he could avoid grieving. In our early weeks together, he showed a gentle vulnerability, an attractive sensitivity. But a tough-guy façade grew more and more prominent. I asked him where my Karl had gone. *"Huh. Past history,"* he mumbled.

When I went in to work each morning, I was myself. I had creative ideas and laughed with co-workers. When Karl and I were alone together or around other people—his friends—I was withdrawn.

Karl would tell me about punching out co-workers who disagreed with him. Karl carried a dangerous energy. Something in me must have wanted a man who didn't question his own motives, a man who got what he wanted. Surely, such a man could provide security to an insecure woman.

It was ownership Karl felt toward me, not love. Humiliation was part of the package. If we went food shopping, he talked loudly, asking if we had enough *"FOOD STAMPS"* to pay for everything. He was never on food stamps. He just enjoyed the shocked looks on other shoppers' faces. The more I blushed, the broader his grin.

Worst of all was his sexual fantasy. Soon after they married, Karl convinced Gretchen to go to a bar with him. She was to pick up a stranger, bring him home, and have sex while Karl watched. She did. They fought afterwards because Gretchen admitted she enjoyed it.

He said I, too, should pick up some guy to prove how much I loved him. He occasionally took me to a local bar. I drank one glass of wine, paid no attention to any man but Karl, then got him to take me home. My job in health care gave me no illusions about the safety of sex with absolute strangers. Karl asked me why I wouldn't play his game. *"That's easy,"* I said, *"I don't want to die of AIDS. "Well,"* he huffed, *"they have drugs for that."* I was certain that love meant you did not put your partner's health or life in danger. Karl didn't care what happened to me as long as he had a good time. The obsession was fast unraveling. When it came undone, there was nothing else. No love. Nothing.

Karl had rifles, shotguns, and pistols stored in various places around the house—some on both floors. I was afraid to tell him I was leaving, so I asked four friends to help me one morning after he left for work. I thought I had escaped when we shoved the last packing box into the rental truck.

Escaped? No. I had only dumped a man as self-centered and immature as I was. I blamed Karl for a long time. Vigorously stirring the drama pot, I kept asking myself how Karl could have done what he did to innocent me. The real question was, *"What is it in me that chose a man like that?"* Even though there was no logical reason for my fear, I had long wondered if I would wind up as a bag lady some day. That was what made me choose him.

If I had been conscious, I would have asked myself several questions before Karl and I got very far into the relationship, such as what he and I could build as partners that neither of us could create as individuals.

The only answer would have been—nothing. How much did Karl and I encourage each other to grow as people? We didn't. I kept his house clean. I cooked. We had sex. We had some laughs. We had no meaningful conversations. I sleepwalked, start to finish. My decisions were all determined by fear or anger. Not one was made consciously. Not one.

D. Growth Practice

- Today, stay conscious of not treating anyone or anyone's ideas with disrespect—not even in your mind. At some point today, consider taking a walk—maybe at lunch.

AFTERNOON

E. Thinking/Journaling

- Write in your journal about one way of negative thinking or acting or speaking or feeling that you would like to conquer— one that has conquered you in the past.

EVENING

F. Consciousness Expansion

- Have you ever made a life decision based on fear, jealousy, the desire to dominate or control, or any other negative emotion that you can identify? How did that turn out?

G. Think About

I'm told that the Inuit people have about 40 words that are all translated into English as "snow." What we speak of as "love" is also many things. To some people, jealousy, possessiveness, and control are intricately connected to their idea of love. I was once so needy that I accepted anyone else's definition of love as my own.

Love, I now know, is a verb. Love is what people do, not what they say, that communicates the depth and the quality of their feelings. What kinds of ongoing actions might tell you that someone loves you? How do you express love as a verb on a daily basis?

Good Night Meditation

Relax completely for a few minutes in silence, eyes closed. Ask yourself what you learned this day, what you shared with another, what you could have done better, and how you can bring yourself into greater alignment with your soul mind.

Perseverance: Day 19

MORNING
Please do A, B, C, and D.

A. Meditation

1. *Invitation*

- Rub your palms together briskly for a few seconds.

- Then, rest your hands, palms up, in your lap or on your thighs.

- Make a circle with thumb and forefinger with the remaining fingers relaxed.

- Sit quietly for a few moments, eyes closed.

- With eyes still closed, raise them to focus on an imaginary small dot in the middle of your forehead. Maintain that focus throughout the meditation. Hold a receptive attitude.

2. *This Day's Intention*

- When you are ready to shift into making your intention, think to yourself:
  For my highest good, I can change; I can learn and unlearn.

- Repeat that thought:
  For my highest good, I can change; I can learn and unlearn.

3. *Releasing and Relaxing*

- After a few moments, release your intention and rest in peaceful, receptive inner connection for a few minutes. Release any thoughts that come up and return to your meditation.

4. *Return*

- When you are ready, take a couple of deep breaths, open your eyes, and bring yourself to full consciousness of where you are.

5. *Start the Day*

- With eyes open, say aloud:
  For my highest good, I can change; I can learn and unlearn.

B. Quotation

We can get carried away by our negative emotions. We may say things we wish we could take back. We do not have to continue living in the same way that we have always lived. Be grateful that learning is a two-way street. You can learn. You can also unlearn.

–The Lecturer

C. Life Story: *Brain Bees*

Looking for evidence that I had managed to persevere after something worthwhile, I usually found just the opposite. When I discovered some kind of continuity in my life, it wasn't necessarily a source of pride.

I became aware of an ongoing "buzz" in my mind. It was the countless irritations, frustrations, and angers that had lived in my head for as long as I could remember. This was more than a tendency to judge or criticize. It had become the river I swam in.

I used to think a negative take on life was an important part of who I was—an internal Mac the Knife, so to speak, but I had begun to change. The bees in my brain no longer fit the me that I was becoming. Besides, I discovered the buzz couldn't make distinctions between dumb stuff and important stuff—I got upset over *anything: "Why is my mail box full of junk?" "Why is there so much corruption?" "Why do I have wrinkles?"* Because most of my complaints were about things I could not change, I had few, if any really sunny days. Even the good days could turn. And often did.

What happened was never my fault, never my responsibility. Maybe I'd stashed some money in a "safe place" and forgotten where. I was sure someone had stolen it—until I found the money. If I got hit with a $40 late fee, it was that greedy credit card company's fault for not giving me a break. If I had just paid the bill on time—but that never occurred to me. If I tore a dress, I blamed it on the dress or on whatever tore it, not on the fact that I wasn't looking where I was going. A speeding ticket was worth a major rant. A flat tire was worse. Sometimes, I could point the finger at myself (the ticket). Sometimes, stuff just happened (the flat tire). Dissatisfaction with the world sang to the dark Muzak® that burbled along in my brain.

In Japan, I felt frustrated because of the inconveniences and difficulties of living abroad. Lots of things work in another culture, but not in the way we think they should. It's easy to find ourselves in "grumble mode" when out of our element. When I finally got back to America, I expected life to be perfect because, well, this is America! It's home.

My definition of perfect was, of course, whatever suited *me*. Nothing should be inconvenient. Every day, I should be greeted by pleasant opportunities to do exactly what I wanted. People should treat me with the respect I deserved. Bosses should pay me every penny I was worth. Reality bit. Why, I wondered, did Americans have to push and shove in their rush to get somewhere? Why do they swipe stuff from each other? Why do I run out of ink? What's *wrong*?

By the time I recognized how much the bees spoiled a part of every day, I had already made some changes—and in significant areas. If you can say you're trying to learn patience, that carries a little cachet. You can give yourself a small gold star for working on arrogance, too. But who wants to admit to a lifelong, mile-deep *whiner* habit? Ewwww! There you have it. Anything that crossed my path could get me going. I was soooo full of myself. Maybe all those angry little emotions made me know I was not just the cotton-candy sweetie on public display.

How could I break such a firmly entrenched habit? Habits are not pussycats. They are tigers. They lie in wait until something triggers the mechanism. They pounce and leave bloody tracks behind them. You don't *play* with habits. So, first, I had to examine my resolve. Did I really want to give up a habit that made me feel better about myself? Acting superior made me feel tall at others' expense. Then, I saw it: Although I wanted a deepening connection with other people, the more I lived like a know-it-all, the less connected I felt. The bees were from outer mind, not soul mind.

I was determined to make myself conscious every time this familiar negative river threatened to carry me off. Simple awareness—without doing anything about it—would be enough at first. I peeled back a corner on my life to see what was crawling around down there.

In the beginning, I noticed my autopilot irritations only a couple of times a day. With attention, awareness grew. I was grumbling from morning until night! To get a handle on my habit, each experience had to be analyzed—along with its root cause. Can't fit into my favorite jeans? Maybe if I opened my mouth less to Haagen-Dazs® and more to veggies

. . . Lost my ticket to a play? Next time, maybe I'll staple tickets into my calendar instead of stuffing them—wherever. Late with taxes? Not the government's fault. How about getting better organized with my constant paper chase? Bashed my head again on the corner of the cupboard door? Maybe if I closed it every time I opened it . . . and so on.

I also wondered, *"Am I ever justified in feeling angry?"* What things *should* I get angry about, and what things should I just let go—or even laugh at? *Laugh* at? I had taken many things about life way too seriously—just so I could complain about them. And if, as the lecturer said, peace truly does begin with me, isn't that an invitation to the dance?

What about principle, though? What about something that's important to us? I got upset, for example, when a friend kept passing along racist e-mails after I asked her not to. But even my anger is different these days. It's not a wildfire that threatens to incinerate the heavens. It's a controlled burn. Recently, I repeated my request about the e-mails. This time, I was not overly polite. I told her how I feel about racism and why. In detail. My stand cost me the friendship. To keep that friend, I would have had to keep my mouth shut about something that's important to me. Years ago, I would have done that without a second thought. Not now.

D. Growth Practice

- Today, keep an eye on any tendency toward going on automatic with negative thinking such as, *"He only cares about himself."* *"She's so dumb." "Why can't I do anything right?"* If you have such thoughts, do they come from a "should"? What might the fear and the reality be?

AFTERNOON

E. Thinking/Journaling

- Most relationships come to a parting of the ways eventually. Have you ever had a relationship with a friend or a family member that got strained or broken? Write about how the problem came about, what happened, and how you feel about it now. How do you think the other person perceives of it? Have you ever really discussed it, or (if you are still together) does it remain off limits? What have you learned?

EVENING

F. Consciousness Expansion

- Standing up courageously and powerfully for principle is one thing. Blowing up at someone's mistake is another. Can you think of an example of each in your life?

G. Think About

Have you ever noticed how people can be unnecessarily rude? Everyday insults are so common we hardly recognize them for what they are anymore. What if we spoke and acted respectfully toward everyone we met—especially toward those who cannot possibly do us any favors? Might that make a difference in our lives?

√ *Look back. How are you doing with discarding an old habit that no longer serves the life you want to live?*

Good Night Meditation

Relax completely for a few minutes in silence, eyes closed. Ask yourself what you learned this day, what you shared with another, what you could have done better, and how you can bring yourself into greater alignment with your soul mind.

Perseverance: Day 20

MORNING
Experience A, B, C, and D.

A. Meditation

1. *Invitation*

- Rub your palms together briskly for a few seconds.

- Then, rest your hands, palms up, in your lap or on your thighs.

- Make a circle with thumb and forefinger with the remaining fingers relaxed.

- Sit quietly for a few moments, eyes closed.

- With eyes still closed, raise them to focus on an imaginary small dot in the middle of your forehead. Maintain that focus throughout the meditation. Hold a receptive attitude.

2. *This Day's Intention*

- When you are ready to shift into making your intention, think to yourself:
  I will not be stubborn.

- Repeat that thought:
  I will not be stubborn.

3. *Releasing and Relaxing*

- After a few moments, release your intention and rest in peaceful, receptive inner connection for a few minutes. Release any thoughts that come up and return to your meditation.

4. *Return*

- When you are ready, take a couple of deep breaths, open your eyes, and bring yourself to full consciousness of where you are.

5. *Start the Day*

- With eyes open, say aloud:
  I will not be stubborn.

B. Quotation

Make up your mind not to be stubborn. Being stubborn is not the same as persevering after a goal. Perseverance sees the big picture. Perseverance allows us to shift direction, depending on circumstances and the highest good of those involved. Stubbornness is outer mind-based. It sees only self and goal. Stubbornness cares for nothing and is moved by nothing.

–The Lecturer

C. Life Story: *Promises to Keep*

Each man I met was "the one," my last chance for happiness. I *had* to make it work. I'd been through two divorces, having learned little from either one. Now, there was Andy who—bless him—adored me. I felt no chemistry with Andy, but I was determined to create that spark by force of will alone. I could be immovable in my stubbornness. I could jam both feet in the stirrups, put blinders on, and leap. This approach had never brought me what I wanted before. With Andy, it would!

Andy proudly admitted that he picked women several notches above him in intelligence and looks. I assumed his humble assessment was just that—and I'd find a deep, secret self inside the simple, kind man. I did look. I did not find. Perhaps I wasn't looking in the right places.

After six months of a platonic relationship, I decided it was time for sex. I already knew we had nothing in common intellectually. I also knew he was a good man, an honest man, a hardworking and loving man. I was so tired of the other kind. I *wanted* to grow in love with him and I was determined to stick with it until we clicked. Sex would turn the key.

He made weekend reservations for us at a beautiful waterside resort in southeastern Virginia. We enjoyed a delicious seafood dinner with wine and candles, followed by a long, meandering walk along the water, hand in hand. It was fairy-tale beautiful. I was nervous. I kicked my butterflies aside.

There were all the little things I didn't like about Andy. He had no sense of style. I told myself I was being shallow. I didn't like his face—especially his nose, eyes, and ears. I told myself his face would grow on me. I didn't like his mannerisms, especially the way he'd pull his chin in, lift both shoulders toward his ears, and grin in a truly doofus manner. It was part of a persona he enjoyed at 50—that of the eternal kid. I told myself I needed to broaden my perspective. Most of all, I disliked the baby talk he constantly used with me. We were wrong for each other from the start and it was only my determination to make something out of nothing that drove us to consummate things that night.

He was lighthearted and happy afterward. I felt lonely and disconnected. Having sex only intensified my growing awareness that you cannot stubbornly force love—especially when both the externals and the internals of a relationship are telling you that nothing's going to happen. Not now. Not ever.

We dated for six more months. He seemed not to mind that we rarely had sex. I was still holding a skinny hope that our enforced togetherness would bring me around. He was such a nice guy.

The lecturer talked once about marriage and how important it is to keep promises. I had promised myself I'd make this relationship work—not realizing that you cannot compel the heart by only engaging mind and body. Asked once if people had to stay married because they'd made a promise, the lecturer replied, *"If a couple is always bickering, what kind of marriage is that? It's no good if all you do is fight."* Andy and I didn't fight, although sometimes I said snotty things to him. He never took the bait. I was in a no-win battle with myself. He was just along for the ride.

Andy took me on a Christmas trip to New York City where we stayed in his daughter's elegant apartment right on Central Park South. Marjorie was beautiful, lively, and bright—with an astounding collection of Prada shoes.

It had just snowed. The city was beautiful in the way that only New York can be while the snow is fresh and clean.

Marjorie, her husband Mark, and I talked comfortably and at length about music, the city, and life. I felt cut off from Andy. On our first night there, Andy and I lay side by side in a double bed, our stomachs full of lobster. I made no overtures toward him—no touching and no kissing. The lights were off. The silence stretched out for miles. He asked what was wrong. The words poured out of me. *"Andy, I'm sorry. You care for me a lot more than I care for you."* He lay still for a few moments, then turned away from me and was soon snoring.

The next morning, we saw Marjorie and Mark off on a trip to the Caribbean. Andy packed and took a taxi to the train station. I stayed on for two more days—as originally planned—all by myself. I was completely happy for the first time in the year and a half since Andy and I met. No longer feeling pressured to fabricate love, I walked for hours, window-shopping, dropping in at museums, and enjoying the smells, the people, and the pace of New York City.

A gentleman to the last, Andy picked me up at the railroad station back in D.C. He asked how the train trip had been, said he'd been busy working, and told me he'd heard from Marjorie. Something was missing. He was no longer using baby talk. It was over.

D. Growth Practice

- If you find yourself stubbornly pushing to get your way or resisting someone else's ideas or plans, consciously weigh what you are doing and why. Is there another way that might work better for all concerned? How about asking someone to join you on a walk today—or for lunch?

AFTERNOON

E. Thinking/Journaling

Choose one of the following:

- Write a page in your journal about a time that you decided to do something no matter what anyone else wanted. How did that turn out? What did you learn?

- Have you ever been on the receiving end of someone else's blindly stubborn determination that you *were* going to do what he or she wanted? What happened? What was it like? How did you deal with it? Is that person still in your life? Do you blame him or her? Did you grow from the experience in any way? How?

EVENING

F. Consciousness Expansion

- How important do you think it is to get buy-in from other people when you work with them on a project (or in a relationship or marriage)? How good are you at doing that? Do you tend to decide how things should be, and then tell others how to do them? Or are you the one who usually gets pushed to do what others want? If you would like to see changes in such interactions, how might you start to bring them about?

G. Think About

Some people will stay in a relationship or a marriage long after it has no spark left. Can people who are living parallel lives bring their love alive again? One author advises troubled couples to focus on each other and cut off any connection with possible third parties until the primary relationship is either healed or ended. What do you think of that idea? What might it accomplish? What might it avoid?

√ *Look back. How patient are you continuing to be with yourself on a daily basis?*

Good Night Meditation

Relax completely for a few minutes in silence, eyes closed. Ask yourself what you learned this day, what you shared with another, what you could have done better, and how you can bring yourself into greater alignment with your soul mind.

Perseverance: Day 21

MORNING
Do A, B, C, and D.

A. Meditation

1. *Invitation*

- Rub your palms together briskly for a few seconds.

- Then, rest your hands, palms up, in your lap or on your thighs.

- Make a circle with thumb and forefinger with the remaining fingers relaxed.

- Sit quietly for a few moments, eyes closed.

- With eyes still closed, raise them to focus on an imaginary small dot in the middle of your forehead. Maintain that focus throughout the meditation. Hold a receptive attitude.

2. *This Day's Intention*

- When you are ready to shift into making your intention, think to yourself:
  I will make my experiences into tools for growth.

- Repeat that thought:
  I will make my experiences into tools for growth.

3. *Releasing and Relaxing*

- After a few moments, release your intention and rest in peaceful, receptive inner connection for a few minutes. Release any thoughts that come up and return to your meditation.

4. *Return*

- When you are ready, take a couple of deep breaths, open your eyes, and bring yourself to full consciousness of where you are.

5. *Start the Day*

- With eyes open, say aloud:
  I will make my experiences into tools for growth.

B. Quotation

> *Our human tendency to procrastinate leads us to miss so much of the richness of life. In Earth School, we use our experiences as tools for growth. By working on our weaknesses, we are fulfilling much of our purpose.*
>
> —The Lecturer

C. Life Story: *Harriet*

Harriet was unique. I've never met anyone who knew more about love than she did. I was one of a group of five women and one man who set aside a year's worth of Tuesday evenings for Harriet's coaching class in Bethesda, Maryland. Harriet never wrote a book and she rarely addressed more than a handful of people at a time. She knew how hard it was for people to change their notions and actions around love, and so she gave it all she had, one person at a time. I think her mission in life was to teach confused singles how to recognize what they did to keep themselves single—or at least unhappy in their singleness—and how to start making changes. As an Imago* therapist, she concentrated on teaching openness, honesty, kindness, and creative ways of interacting.

My ideas around love tended to be dark and me-centered. Harriet's love was neither. She loved all six of us—her dysfunctional ducklings—unconditionally. She was respectful, supportive—a cheerleader for the smallest green evidence of personal growth.

The lecturer once said that people who claim to fall in and out of love don't even know what love is. Harriet would have agreed. Once Harriet loved you, that was it. Her love energy was powerful, cleansing, healing. She taught unconditional love and she lived what she taught.

Harriet told us about an afternoon spent with an old friend when the two of them were walking to a supermarket to pick up ingredients for lunch at Harriet's. Marilyn was complaining about how unfriendly Southerners were. Harriet grinned. *"Let's experiment. At the store, you pick up the first half of what's on the shopping list. I'll pick up the second half. Both of us will shop the way we usually do, deal?"*

---

*Imago coaching was developed by Harville Hendrix, PhD, author of *Getting the Love You Want* and *Keeping the Love You Find*.

Wheeling the shopping basket smartly through the aisles, Marilyn tossed in bread, cheese, fruit, and crackers. *"Okay,"* said Harriet, *"my turn."* Harriet rolled the basket toward a huge bin of fresh corn. A middle-aged woman was fingering the golden harvest. Harriet spoke. *"Excuse me. How do you pick out good corn?"* The woman looked up, surprised, into Harriet's smiling face. Harriet was advised to pull back a portion of the husk and look for plenty of fresh, plump kernels. *"You really know corn,"* said Harriet. *"Are you from the Midwest?"* The woman's eyes lit up. *"As a matter of fact I am—Iowa."* Harriet said, *"I knew it! You have the air of a woman who understands produce. Do you still have family in Iowa?"* Soon, the two women were chatting about children and grandchildren.

Their conversation over, Harriet wished the woman well and they parted. Harriet kept finding people to talk to, aisle after aisle. A trip to the supermarket with Harriet took a lot longer than it takes most of us. Harriet wasn't focused on getting in and getting out. Or shopping. Time wasn't money. Time spent with people could not be wasted. During those moments, those brief conversations, no one on Earth was more important to Harriet than the people that she would probably never meet again. Harriet chose to go against her early beginnings, to live with courage and love and humor, instead of fear and isolation. She met friendly people because that's what she embodied and that's what she expected. She knew no strangers. Literally.

Harriet never sugarcoated the hard work it took for both partners to win on the field of love. And she would flash her brown eyes at the idea that love didn't require effort. *"Give me one reason why not!"* said Harriet. It was a lot like gardening, she told us. Love takes conscious daily watering, pruning, and fertilizing.

As a child, Harriet told us, she never believed she deserved happiness. She consciously transformed herself. Harriet and John had a marriage that the rest of us could only admire and dream of. Since we weren't Harriet or John, we couldn't have what they had. But, oh, what a light they shone!

By focusing on their "non-negotiables,"—those things that both partners had to have in a relationship—Harriet and John identified what became the rock on which their marriage was built. They had a common passion for integrity and outreach. They had the guts and consistency it took to work toward ever-deeper intimacy with one another. *"Speak from the heart,"* Harriet told us. *"Don't be afraid of being vulnerable to the person you love. That's where you connect—that's how you connect."*

I had walked into a whole new world. You mean we have choices? And our choices lead somewhere predictable?

I so wanted to follow in Harriet's footsteps. I could not. First of all, I wasn't ready to connect with a partner. I needed to work on my own stuff, stuff I couldn't even identify at the time. I habitually procrastinated. I put off the need to change and grow beyond where I was. Fearful and lazy, I continued to tread water and wonder why life hurt so much.

I was planning to stay with Harriet until what she was rubbed off on me. I might still be there, nodding my head, taking notes, feeling inspired, and making no perceptible life changes. Harriet died, much too early, of ovarian cancer. If I wanted transformation, I'd have to look somewhere else.

I've sought angels all my life, male or female—looking for someone who could do for me what I could not or would not do for myself. That continued until I finally understood this truth, a truth fundamental to the human condition: No one here, there, or anywhere else can do the work for us. That's because it's not theirs to do.

D. Growth Practice

- Most of us can use some conscious work around how we interact with others. Some have difficulty getting to places on time. Others are married to time. Some save their most cutting remarks for the people they supposedly love best. If these scenarios don't ring a bell, how about looking at the way you treat yourself? Find a way to spend some gentle time in Nature today—maybe with someone else or maybe alone.

AFTERNOON

E. Thinking/Journaling

- Write about how difficult it was to make a hard decision in your life. What guides you at such times? What would a conscious approach as you understand it add to your decision-making? Can you think of an example?

EVENING

F. Consciousness Expansion

- How much can you see the effects of procrastination when you look around you—not only in your home, but at work, and on a larger scale? Can you think of something you wanted but missed out on because of procrastination? Could now be the time to get a handle on the tendency to put things off?

G. Think About

Is there someone, famous or not famous, whose way of living has so impressed you that it changed your life? Is there a saying that you memorized because it inspired you? We are surrounded by angels (and not all of them look like angels). Who or what are yours—and why?

√ *Look back. Can you imagine expressing unconditional love, a love that embraces others not for what they do for us, but for who they really are? Would you like to try?*

Good Night Meditation

Relax completely for a few minutes in silence, eyes closed. What did you learn today? What did you share with someone else? What could you have done better? How can you deepen your connection with your soul mind?

Chapter Twelve
Workbook: On Adaptability

You are at a singles' party, standing near a table piled with cheese and crackers. A stranger walks up, reaches for a snack, and smiles at you. If you're on autopilot and you are a woman hoping to meet a man, your reaction probably depends largely on the gender of the smiler.

If it's another woman, you may meet her eyes and nod briefly. She's competition. She's also distracting you from your goal. Some other woman could snag your dream guy while you're exchanging comments about . . . what? The cheese? The host or hostess? The décor? She's probably only smiling to be polite, anyway. She's checking out your hair (too short and too brassy), your dress (too tight, wrong color), and your heels (too old—you know you should have worn the new ones even if they do hurt).

If you are reacting unconsciously, the odor of imagined criticism pushes you clear across the room. You don't need *her* to tell *you* what's wrong with *you*! Her dress isn't all that great, either. And she could afford to lose a few pounds. You have no time for her or any other woman at this party. If you could, you'd wave a wand and all the other women would disappear. You need a man. A man will complete you. The sooner you find him, the sooner you'll feel fully alive again.

If you are responding consciously, however, the gender of the smiler won't matter. You'll offer a smile of your own (unless there's a good reason not to). You may start off with small talk. It may go nowhere. Or you may wind up forming a friendship—with a man or a woman—that will warm your heart for years. Maybe for a lifetime.

When I was trying to come up with an image to describe adaptability, I pictured myself standing at this party completely surrounded, head to toe, by a metal cylinder that others could not see. If I refused to be flexible in my thoughts, words, feelings, and actions, all I saw was the inside of the cylinder's highly mirrored surface. Actually, all that cylinder reflected was my fixed ideas about other people and myself. All I felt was fear and doubt. All I saw was stereotypes.

The minute I chose to "vaporize" the cylinder, I could see—and respond to—a world of fresh possibilities.

Step into those possibilities now with Day 22's meditation on adaptability.

Adaptability: Day 22

MORNING
Please complete A, B, C, and D.

A. Meditation

1. *Invitation*

- Rub your palms together briskly for a few seconds.

- Then, rest your hands, palms up, in your lap or on your thighs.

- Make a circle with thumb and forefinger with the remaining fingers relaxed.

- Sit quietly for a few moments, eyes closed.

- With eyes still closed, raise them to focus on an imaginary small dot in the middle of your forehead. Maintain that focus for nine or ten minutes. Hold a receptive attitude.

2. *This Day's Intention*

- When you are ready to shift into making your intention, think to yourself:
  I will practice the art of adaptability.

- Repeat that thought:
  I will practice the art of adaptability.

3. *Releasing and Relaxing*

- After a few moments, release your intention and rest in peaceful, receptive inner connection for a minute or two. Release thoughts of past or future that may arise and return to your meditation.

4. *Return*

- When you are ready, take a couple of deep breaths, open your eyes, and bring yourself back to your outer life.

5. *Start the Day*

- With eyes open, say aloud:
  I will practice the art of adaptability.

B. Quotation

> In life, we often find ourselves in circumstances that we
> do not like and never, ever would have consciously chosen to
> experience. At those times, we are called on to practice the art of
> adaptability.   -The Lecturer

C. Life Story: *Fired*

I have been fired three times. Each time was devastating—none more than the first. I'd been co-anchoring at WGHP-TV in North Carolina for four years when the station was sold. The new owner started cleaning house from the top—starting with the general manager. I was number eight on his list. I wondered if it was because I was then 45. Now, I believe I wanted to avoid facing the truth: I was a very average anchor. The station replaced me with someone who worked harder than I did at both news-gathering and at embodying the larger-than-life image of an anchor.

The new general manager canned me after the 6 p.m. news one night. I had assumed I'd be WGHP's co-anchor until I fell over dead one day at my desk. Now, that wasn't going to happen. I was too busy blaming the new owner to learn anything from the experience. Blaming him allowed me to believe he was wrong and I was right, so I did not use that opportunity to change. That set me up to get fired a second time.

Two years later, I went to work in Pennsylvania for a medical television production facility that created short syndicated TV news stories on health and medicine. The stories were sold to smaller television stations that couldn't afford health reporters. My new job required familiarity with a vast amount of medical and scientific material and a highly organized approach. I was disorganized and out of my depth—and knew it.

A few weeks after I started, the company sent me to San Francisco to host a videotaping of a season's worth of half-hour programs with local MDs—on 22 different medical topics. I was terrified. At WGHP, the script scrolled before my eyes on a teleprompter as I spoke—no need to memorize anything. Here, there were no teleprompters. I stayed up very late the night before the taping, cramming information into my head. Fear of failure made it fly right out again. In desperation, I scribbled notes to myself on small pieces of paper. I scattered those notes all over my desk, begging the cameraman, *"Stay on my face. Please don't show my notes."* He nodded. Watching videos of those shows weeks later, I was mortified. There I was, parked behind a dark desk that looked like it had been caught in a severe paper snowstorm.

Since way back when we were dodging carnivorous dinosaurs, we humans have reacted to danger by fighting, fleeing, or freezing. I froze. The real problem wasn't with the scraps of paper. It was with me. In my terror, I sat ab-so-lute-ly still on camera. Picture a mummy who speaks. I wasn't *that* bad. But close.

If I had not been operating out of a myth—that I should already know everything about everything—I would have asked for more time to prepare. It was all about *me*. My complicated questions for the doctors were designed to show off my little brain, not to bring forth answers to questions the viewers might have asked. Viewers' needs never even registered. I was inflexible. In my mind, there was only one way to do things—my way.

Again, I blamed the man who did the firing. After all, I had never bent my proud neck to laugh at any of his jokes. Obviously, he was mean-spirited and vindictive. A complex personality, he was an easy target—much easier than the real reason.

The third time I got fired was at a hospital in Pennsylvania. My job there as the staff writer grew boring. When the hospital's production coordinator quit, I asked for a transfer. To do that job well, I needed stone-cold familiarity with the printing business. I needed the discipline to set up a comprehensive tracking schedule for the many interlocking steps required to get all of the hospital's publications out on time. I should have had the kind of personality that can pleasantly irritate people into meeting deadlines. None of those requirements spoke to my strengths—only to my weaknesses. In less than a year, I was let go. Did I learn anything? A little. Finally. After all, I'd been the one who'd chosen to leap from safety into hell.

The first two firings frayed my golden girl aura. The third one broke it. Permanently. Were all the good things that had happened in my life just flukes? Maybe I wasn't very talented at—anything. I felt battered, confused, and filled with despair.

Moving to Virginia, I took a job as a part-time editorial assistant with a small association—a job with so few demands that I could not fail. Later, a secretarial position came open there. I took it—just because it was full time. My plan was to stay in my little corner, do my little job, and remain with that association. Forever. I did the same work in the same way every day—and recoiled from opportunities that might have led to growth. I took home my tiny paycheck and scraped by, sometimes reliving the good old on-camera days to have any sense of myself. I had become a nobody with no future, just a past. After four years with the association, I was reborn during the night of *taiko* drumming at the Smithsonian. That was the night I rediscovered passion. And hope.

D. Growth Practice

- Keep your eyes open today for opportunities to learn from and adapt to what's going on around you without getting irritated or upset by it. Try to remember that reality is what it is. What's important is how you respond to it and what you learn.

AFTERNOON

E. Thinking/Journaling

Choose one of the following:

- Write about a time that you felt rejected, or a time that you lost a job. What happened? Did you grow through the experience?

- Think back to when you blamed someone else for a bad experience. If you look closely, can you see your contribution to the problem?

EVENING

F. Consciousness Expansion

- In what ways do you believe that greater flexibility on your part might improve your life? How might you start working in that direction?

G. Think About

Getting fired could have taught me some important lessons if I'd been open to them. Extreme experiences bring us face to face with possibilities for making great strides in life. They can be frightening or shattering. They may turn us in a totally different life direction from the one we thought we wanted. Experiences like that are always valuable—if we use them well.

√ *Look back. Do you find that any of your interactions with others and with yourself are improving? In what ways?*

Good Night Meditation

Relax completely for a few minutes in silence, eyes closed. What did you learn today? What did you share with someone else? What could you have done better? How can you deepen your connection with your soul mind?

Adaptability: Day 23

MORNING
Do A, B, C, and D.

A. Meditation

1. *Invitation*

- Rub your palms together briskly for a few seconds.

- Then, rest your hands, palms up, in your lap or on your thighs.

- Make a circle with thumb and forefinger with the remaining fingers relaxed.

- Sit quietly for a few moments, eyes closed.

- With eyes still closed, raise them to focus on an imaginary small dot in the middle of your forehead. Maintain that focus for nine or ten minutes. Hold a receptive attitude. Do not worry about what it is that you receive.

2. *This Day's Intention*

- When you are ready to shift into making your intention, think to yourself:
  I will regularly take inventory of my emotions, thoughts, and desires.

- Repeat:
  I will regularly take inventory of my emotions, thoughts, and desires.

3. *Releasing and Relaxing*

- After a few moments, release your intention and rest in peaceful, receptive inner connection for a minute or two. Release thoughts of past or future that may arise and return to your meditation.

4. *Return*

- When you are ready, take a couple of deep breaths, open your eyes, and bring yourself back to your outer life.

5. *Start the Day*

- With eyes open, say aloud:
  I will regularly take inventory of my emotions, thoughts, and desires.

B. Quotation

> Take inventory of your emotions, thoughts, and desires. update yourself on where you are in life. Don't expect to quickly or easily overcome what you've been doing habitually for years. You can't. That would be nothing short of a miracle, and I don't believe in miracles. When you inventory your thoughts, you may say, "Now, I see where I am wrong—that what I do is wrong. I am making myself miserable."
>
> —The Lecturer

C. Life Story: *The Commute*

For years, I dreaded my morning commute. All those other drivers in northern Virginia had no business on the road. They were dangerous, stupid, and slow. They made me late to work. When I drove to the office, I never gave pedestrians a break. If I could squeak past them in my rush to get where I was going, I did.

I looked forward to my commute when traffic thinned—on the few holidays that our office didn't observe, and during the summer. On those days, I could zip in to the office almost on time. That was how it should be *every* day, I thought. It wasn't. And no matter how hard I held on to how it should be, I could not change what was.

I drove to work angry, arrived at work angry, rushed to my desk still angry. *"I hate Metro traffic!"* I announced to everyone and no one. Or I'd mumble, *"bad traffic,"* *"accident,"* or *"The cat ate my alarm clock."* It never occurred to me that everyone in the office faced the same traffic and most of them made it to the office on time—or at least earlier than I did.

Clocking the distance from home to office, I found it was a perfect 11-minute commute. In my mind, that's what it *should* be, no matter what. So that's what I allowed. Not a minute more. I was a hard worker. It was okay to stay late at the office. It was not okay to leave home earlier to get to the office. Not one of my morning minutes had anyone's name on it but mine. An 11-minute commute was an 11-minute commute—rain, shine, snow, summer, or winter. And it shouldn't matter that the day I clocked that first 11-minute commute was a Sunday!

Poring over city maps, I devised a dozen different routes between home and office. Some were faster, some slower. They all took at least 20 minutes on weekdays. I stuck to my guns. Surely, there was a secret route.

At last, I accepted that there really was no "northwest passage" between home and office. I continued to arrive late. I continued to hate my commute.

One morning, as I moved unhappily into heavy traffic, a thought popped up: *"What if I left for the office ten minutes early?"* What? Ridiculous idea. I honked with irritation at the woman sleep-driving in front of me.

In the days to come, that thought returned. No! Early? Never! Finally, I tried it. It was like melted butter—the commute was that smooth. I got in to work with a couple of minutes to spare. My co-workers looked up in surprise as I smiled my way down the hall, steaming cup of coffee in hand.

That wasn't the only change I made. I began to treat my fellow drivers better—even letting some of them cut in ahead of me (poor things, they must have gotten up late, I thought—or maybe they didn't allow enough time for their commute). Now, I graciously allowed pedestrians the right to cross the streets in safety. *"After you!"*

With my ten-minute cushion, I could head out with music in my ears (I'd stopped listening to the news, which was only death and destruction, anyway), knowing that even if all the lights turned red, even if someone had a fender bender, even if every other driver on the road turned out to be more stupid than I was, I would arrive on time. Or early.

The more I did it, the more I liked it. In the end, I was leaving 10 minutes early every morning—even 15. I was courteous, kind, smiling, and happy all the way to work. I had fit myself into the reality of the situation—streets filled with busy, complex traffic patterns. It was so simple. Why had it taken me so long? I must have wanted to be angry, miserable, stressed, and caught up in my drama. Otherwise, I wouldn't have kept on doing it, right?

D. Growth Practice

- Today, consider looking at a relationship that isn't as smooth as you would like it to be. What is it that really bothers you? Could you be creative about dealing with it? Look for a "should" that may be making things more difficult for you.

Build some time into your schedule today to go for a walk and connect with your inner self.

AFTERNOON

E. Thinking/Journaling

- In your journal, write about a time in your life when you realized that you needed to change your expectations or your hopes toward someone or something. What happened? Which "should" was in operation at that time?

EVENING

F. Consciousness Expansion

- As your own best friend, take a look at some of the things you do that keep you from feeling at peace in your life. Give yourself some good, workable advice. Would an attitude change help? Will you try to stay conscious about this?

G. Think About

When I first moved into my condo, I got very annoyed when I realized that my unit was directly over the automatic garage door to my building. Day and night, residents were driving in and out, in and out. The noise was a constant irritation. And even when everything was quiet, I was on edge in anticipation of the next time that the big door would grind its way open—and grind its way closed. Because the noise wasn't going to go away (and I wasn't going to move), I had to reframe the situation. So I decided that when I heard the door, I would think, *"Good. There's another resident now safely home."* It was a simple way to respond to the situation. It worked.

Good Night Meditation

Relax completely for a few minutes in silence, eyes closed. What did you learn today? What did you share with someone else? What could you have done better? How can you deepen your connection with your soul mind?

Adaptability: Day 24

MORNING
Do A, B, C, and D.

A. Meditation

1. *Invitation*

- Rub your palms together briskly for a few seconds.

- Then, rest your hands, palms up, in your lap or on your thighs.

- Make a circle with thumb and forefinger with the remaining fingers relaxed.

- Sit quietly for a few moments, eyes closed.

- With eyes still closed, raise them to focus on an imaginary small dot in the middle of your forehead. Maintain that focus for nine or ten minutes. Hold a receptive attitude. Do not worry about what it is that you receive.

2. *This Day's Intention*

- When you are ready to shift into making your intention, think to yourself:
  To balance my life, I will adapt to everything that comes my way.

- Repeat:
  To balance my life, I will adapt to everything that comes my way.

3. *Releasing and Relaxing*

- After a few moments, release your intention and rest in peaceful, receptive inner connection for a minute or two. Release thoughts of past or future that may arise and return to your meditation.

4. *Return*

- When you are ready, take a couple of deep breaths, open your eyes, and bring yourself back to your outer life.

5. *Start the Day*

- With eyes open, say aloud:
  To balance my life, I will adapt to everything that comes my way.

B. Quotation

> Balance your life on earth. The only way you can do that
> is through adapting yourself to conditions as they arise, and
> in being able to accept everything that comes into your life.
> Nothing comes to you that is not vital to your growth.
>
> —The Lecturer

C. Life Story: *Past Is Present*

When I was maybe eight, I got nailed for a crime. My teacher caught on that I'd copied the answers to a string of tedious arithmetic questions from the back of my textbook. If I'd included some mistakes, I'd have gotten away with it, but I was too busy being perfect—even while cheating. In front of the whole class, Miss Lang made me an object lesson. I forgave neither her nor the world of numbers.

Years later, I attended a week-long conflict management workshop in Washington, D.C. The instructor passed out several photocopied pages that contained only long columns of numbers—and told us to add them up. He didn't say why. What did this have to do with conflict management? Maybe he wanted to find out if we would robotically do what he said. Or maybe he thought the sight of all those numbers would bring forth a conflict that needed managing. If that was the case, I was up for it.

Looking around, I saw that I was the only one not hunched over those columns. I called the instructor over and whispered that I didn't *like* numbers. Never *had*. Never *would*. And—my heart was pounding wildly—*I wasn't going to do the assignment!*

Joshua Phillips was a bull-shouldered man with a head full of thick, white hair, a bushy white mustache, and large square teeth. He grinned broadly. Leaning close to my ear, he whispered back: *"S-t-r-e-t-c-h!"*

The word shocked me. It wasn't what I expected. I thought he would let me off. As I sat there, thinking, I realized that the numbers were meaningless. What counted was the way I chose to handle them. This was the first time I had even considered growing past my decades-long pissiness because of a teacher I disliked—and who felt the same way about me. I thought my likes and dislikes were a part of who I was.

Maybe I was mistaken. I might never learn to *like* numbers, but did I have to go through life with an automatic negative emotional charge on them? Did memories of Miss Lang have to rule that part of my life? I picked up my pen and slowly began to add up the columns.

During the last three years of my mother's life, I was visiting her twice a week in her assisted care facility. Most of the time, we would talk or I would read to her. When she was focused on the present, it was good. Sometimes, though, her inner eyes reeled her back into ancient hurts. She'd angrily tell me the same family stories she'd been repeating ever since I was a child—stories of rejection and neglect.

I decided to point out the obvious: She had outlived everyone who did any of these things to her. What did it matter anymore? Why not let it go? She listened. She did not hear. Those ancient grudges were welded into place. That old pain was *hers*.

Much later, I realized that I still held old grudges of my own. It does little good to advise someone else—especially your mother—to grow beyond where you are.

D. Growth Practice

- For today, no matter what happens, try not to get hooked into blaming someone else for anything. If you feel upset, try to find the lesson the situation holds for you. Just for practice, hold on to your emotions long enough before expressing them so you can choose a conscious response.

AFTERNOON

E. Thinking/Journaling
Choose one of the following:

- Do you know anyone who holds old grudges? Or who cannot/ will not forgive someone else, or who blames "them" for something *("They" keep a woman in her place. "They" only hire their own kind. "They" won't let me be...do...)* Write a page about what you think such an unconscious angry approach brings to the quality of life.

- Is there someone you blame for something? Has this changed your life in some way? Do you have to continue to hold those emotions in place? Could you find a way to move on? Write a page about this in your journal.

EVENING

F. Consciousness Expansion

- Look for ways to stretch. If you always go to work along the same roads, change your route or your transportation (allow plenty of time for doing the unfamiliar and for surprises along the way). If you always hold the soap in your right hand in the shower, switch to the left. If you towel off from top to bottom, try bottom to top. Adapt wherever you can. Notice how impossible it is to go on autopilot when you're doing things in a new way.

G. Think About

Someone has suggested looking at the five people closest to us—and writing down what most irritates us about them. That's because at the heart of those irritations lie some of our own most valuable lessons. Do we get irritated when friends are full of themselves? Greedy? Selfish? Lazy? Do we get upset at people who don't want to participate in our love of stirring the drama pot?

√ *Look back. How consciously aware have you become of opportunities for learning as your life unfolds?*

Good Night Meditation

Relax completely for a few minutes in silence, eyes closed. What did you learn today? What did you share with someone else? What could you have done better? How can you deepen your connection with your soul mind?

Adaptability: Day 25

MORNING
Please do A, B, C, and D.

A. Meditation

1. *Invitation*

- Rub your palms together briskly for a few seconds.

- Then, rest your hands, palms up, in your lap or on your thighs.

- Make a circle with thumb and forefinger with the remaining fingers relaxed.

- Sit quietly for a few moments, eyes closed.

- With eyes still closed, raise them to focus on an imaginary small dot in the middle of your forehead. Maintain that focus throughout the meditation. Hold a receptive attitude. Do not worry about what it is that you receive.

2. *This Day's Intention*

- When you are ready to shift into making your intention, think to yourself:
Everyone is my teacher.

- Repeat:
Everyone is my teacher.

3. *Releasing and Relaxing*

- After a few moments, release your intention and rest in peaceful, receptive inner connection for a minute or two. Release thoughts of past or future that may arise and return to your meditation.

4. *Return*

- When you are ready, take a couple of deep breaths, open your eyes, and bring yourself back to your outer life.

5. *Start the Day*

- With eyes open, say aloud:
Everyone is my teacher.

B. Quotation

> You will have a better time than you think while learning your lessons. You are in the right place, wherever you are That doesn't mean that you have to remain there forever. Adapt yourself to circumstances. By being flexible, you will accomplish what you should accomplish—and you'll prepare yourself to go on to the next stage of growth. That effort will bring you better health, a better state of mind, and greater success.
> —The Lecturer

C. Life Story: *Illegally Creative*

On the way home from work one afternoon, a police car pulled up behind me. Three blocks from home, he popped his siren twice and flipped on his flashers. I stopped.

Wraparound dark glasses in place, he demanded my license, saying the stickers on my license plate were out of date. I told him the new ones had not come in the mail, so what was a girl to do? I smiled. About then, I remembered that two years earlier, the same thing had happened—and *that* cop had sweetly let me off. I smiled again. This cop, however, had no sense of humor. And no soft spot for females at the mercy of bureaucratic incompetence. He wrote me a *ticket* and then he told me to go home, lock up my car, and not drive again until I was legal. Well, I *had* to get to work in the morning, and I *had* to get back to my townhouse at the end of the day. I couldn't sit around waiting for a pair of stickers!

Back at the complex, I walked around, looking at stickers on other cars. Some were good for another year—those had red numbers on a yellow background. The ones that were good for the next two years all had black numbers on a white background. Hmm. I had just bought my first computer—a Macintosh. Rummaging around in my apartment, I grabbed a ruler and ran back outside to measure the size of the numbers. I cranked up my computer, set everything up and hit "print." Suddenly, there they were—two sets of perfectly forged license plate stickers! Feeling seriously wicked, I cut them down to size. The real stickers were sort of shiny. I wrapped mine in plastic and stuck them onto my license plates with double-sided tape. Smiling, I compared the legal cars in the parking lot with mine. You'd need good eyes to spot the difference.

I headed for work the next morning. No cop. I drove home that night. No cop. I contacted the state capital's sticker makers and was told mine would be in the mail soon.

One afternoon, the sun low on the horizon, I got on the road for home. By now, I'd half forgotten that I was driving around with forged stickers. The hairs on the back of my neck stood up. A cop was in my rearview mirror. He had on those dark glasses and a face that hadn't cracked a smile since the last Ice Age. Every turn I made, he did the same. My armpits were soaked. No matter how I tried to think of an excuse, nothing came to mind. I hadn't forged those stickers because my IQ was 14. Do they toss you in prison for this kind of thing? The signal at the next intersection turned red and I gently stepped on the brakes, stopping just behind another car. There I sat, my rearview mirror filled with Cop Presence.

Idly, my eyes dropped to the stickers on the car in front of me and my heart began to bang wildly against my ribcage. That car's stickers had something my fakes didn't—little glass beads that reflected light. *That's* why the real stickers had been shiny. Mine just had some plastic on them. The light changed and traffic started moving again. My brain told me that when the sun dropped completely below the horizon, you'd need those glass beads to see the numbers on the stickers—and the last rays of sunlight were disappearing. I hadn't been caught before now because I hadn't been driving at night! I could almost hear the cell door slam shut when—the cop made a right-hand turn. I almost passed out with relief.

Now, I will say that the cop who wrote the ticket was a little too rule-bound for me. He was right, though. I should have noticed my out-of-date stickers. I'm fairly obsessive about that now. The reason I included this story is to show that we human beings can adapt even when we think we can't. I am a most unlikely lawbreaker. I can't even tell a decent lie because my face turns red. So this was not like the me that I knew. For some reason, I hadn't been afraid to experiment. I was focused on the problem at hand and a creative solution burst forth. This is what the experience taught me: As long as fear is left out of the equation, creativity is free to come to the rescue. And anyone can act as your creativity teacher—even a hard-nosed cop.

I don't recommend doing what I did. I'm talking theory here, not criminality. If I'd gotten caught, I wouldn't be smiling about it. I hope I didn't attract any sticker karma. If I did, though, this crazy story was almost worth it—almost!

D. Growth Practice

- Today, try something that's a stretch for you. If you think you're no good at art, sit down and try to draw or paint. If you feel like creating an abstract representation of whatever you are looking at, do that. If you like jazz, and not classical music, consider going to a music store and asking one of the salespeople what classical music he or she would recommend to someone with a jazz background. Just try something new to you in art or music. Or read a couple pages of philosophy. Tangle with a math problem. If you find this hard to do, try to identify the "should" that stands in your way. Look for the fear and the reality, as well.

AFTERNOON

E. Thinking/Journaling

Choose one of the following:

- Write about the most creative way you have ever approached a problem. What did you learn from the experience?

- Write about the most creative solution to a problem you've ever seen someone else come up with. What made it so memorable?

EVENING

F. Consciousness Expansion

- Consider changing your evening ritual. If you wear your shoes at home, put on your slippers, instead. If you comb your hair to the left, comb it to the right. Or find some other way to move outside habit. Read a book or call a friend if you usually spend the evening watching TV or at the computer.

G. Think About

Take an hour to go back through some of your earlier entries in the journal. What things stand out? What have you discovered? Where are you going in life?

√ *Look back. How well are you continuing to adapt to unforeseen
circumstances (especially the ones you don't particularly like)?*

Good Night Meditation

Relax completely for a few minutes in silence, eyes closed. What did
you learn today? What did you share with someone else? What could
you have done better? How can you deepen your connection with your
soul mind?

Adaptability: Day 26

MORNING
Please do A, B, C, and D.

A. Meditation

1. *Invitation*

- Rub your palms together briskly for a few seconds.

- Then, rest your hands, palms up, in your lap or on your thighs.

- Make a circle with thumb and forefinger with the remaining fingers relaxed.

- Sit quietly for a few moments, eyes closed.

- With eyes still closed, raise them to focus on an imaginary small dot in the middle of your forehead. Maintain that focus throughout the meditation. Hold a receptive attitude. Do not worry about what it is that you receive.

2. *This Day's Intention*

- When you are ready to shift into making your intention, think to yourself:
  I weigh my fixed ideas to discover if they still serve me.

- Repeat that thought:
  I weigh my fixed ideas to discover if they still serve me.

3. *Releasing and Relaxing*

- After a few moments, release your intention and rest in peaceful, receptive inner connection for a minute or two. Release thoughts of past or future that may arise and return to your meditation.

4. *Return*

- When you are ready, take a couple of deep breaths, open your eyes, and bring yourself back to your outer life.

5. *Start the Day*

- With eyes open, say aloud:
  I weigh my fixed ideas to discover if they still serve me.

B. Quotation

Take the time to weigh your fixed ideas, those ideas about yourself or others that you hold onto, the ones that keep you stuck in place. These ideas tell you, "I am a certain kind of person and I will always be this kind of person." Outer mind may tell you that you never change, but you know you aren't the same person you were ten years ago. That's true of everyone. Could you have changed in important ways—even while telling yourself you're the same? Look inside for evidence of changes in attitude. The search may surprise you.

–The Lecturer

C. Life Story: *Dirt*

She'd been my closest female friend for a quarter of a century. So when Betsy was on her way for a visit from the East Coast, I ran around tidying up and planning fun things to share.

The day before she left for home, Betsy offered to clean the living room while I cooked. For me, that would have been a ten-minute tour with the vacuum. Betsy soon had a corner of my living room rug lifted high, her blue eyes wide and unbelieving at my vast dust bunny collection. I laughed uncomfortably. *"You know that old saying, 'to sweep something under the rug'? That's what rugs are for!"* Her scowl stayed put.

Betsy is a clean fiend. She has fired several maids because they didn't meet her standards. I, however, keep the place just clean enough to suit me—and my standards are not very high.

Taking a deep breath, Betsy told me I "deserved" to have a housekeeper come in once a month to do a deep clean. I felt mildly angry and defensive. Since I was trying to lead a more enlightened life, I decided to keep a lid on it. Pretending you don't feel what you feel, however, is hardly enlightened. The truth? I resented that she, a temporary visitor, was telling me, the permanent resident, what to do with my house.

Later, I informed Betsy that on the day before her next scheduled visit in two years, I'd hire someone to muck out the place. We both laughed the unhappy laughter of two old friends who've agreed not to disagree.

I read about a family once whose house was so filthy it stank all the way to the street. Rather than clean it up, they burned it to the ground. I'm nowhere near that bad. Still, most of the time, mounds of clean laundry are waiting to be put away, dishes need to go in the dishwasher, and the dust builds.

My fixed ideas about housecleaning had been fixed for a very long time. I saw myself as a messy person—even though I don't really *like* living in a messy house. If I didn't make a change now, when would I? After I was dead, maybe?

When the lecturer advised us to "get your house in order," I always thought he meant it *figuratively*. A messy house is *literally* out of order. Mine's never been completely in order for more than a week at a time. This isn't anything I've wanted others to know. The lecturer said there are no secrets—people already know what we most want to hide. Could that be true? I can hardly ask you to keep my secret now, can I?

Why do I live like this? I function well out in the world. I'm not crazy, so *why*? Finally, it came out in my journal, *"By filling my space with physical mess, I can ignore my mental and emotional mess. I use chaos to distract myself, to give my mind something to look at, and feel at the mercy of—I become a helpless victim of myself."*

Sitting with my spiritual journal for a few moments, I wrote down what came to mind about messiness and me. I found one "shouldn't" and one "should":

> *I shouldn't have to clean up after myself.*
> *I should do what I want to do.*

Maybe with the first one, I thought someone else should clean up after me? That made no sense. And the second one was too egotistical to waste time thinking about. The reality was that the outer mind child was still driving this part of my life car. How embarrassing! So what now? In the past, I would have created a string of carrots to get me to do what I didn't want to do, treats I could have if I met my clean-up goal—an hour of reading or an hour-long massage. That's kid stuff, though. It's easily sidestepped.

Taking care of my own space is one of the keys to the fundamental changes I want to make. It's not a worthy philanthropic effort or a major ecological shift. Keeping my space livable would, however, help me break some assumptions I tend to live by. Why do I think I have to keep doing things the way I've always done them? It's a small issue with a large footprint in my life. It's like the "small stuff" I'm asking you to work with.

It's time for me to walk my talk. Whether I enjoy that walk doesn't matter. But the practice, ah, the practice!

D. Growth Practice

- Do you do things you like first, instead of the things that need to be done? Or do you do the reverse? What's your "should"? Will you try the opposite just for today?

AFTERNOON

E. Thinking/Journaling:
Choose one of the following:

- What activity or way of thinking do you think you have kept as a secret from the world? Write about its history and why you continue to hide it.

- If you don't have a dust bunny collection, what else in your life could do with some patient, persistent attention—and a little adaptability?

EVENING

F. Consciousness Expansion

- Do you ever feel like a victim of a bad habit? What would you like to do about that?

G. Think About

I know people who regularly steam-clean their carpets. Every day, they scrub out the sink and put stuff where it belongs. I used to tell myself that those people were wasting their time—they should wait until the messes are so messy and the dust so high that a good cleaning makes a real difference! You may not have a dirt problem. But you're human, so you do have a problem of some kind that you'd just as soon ignore. Whatever it is, take a close look at it and see if you might not be ready to treat it a little (or a lot) differently in the interest of aligning outer mind and soul mind.

Good Night Meditation

Relax completely for a few minutes in silence, eyes closed. What did you learn today? What did you share with someone else? What could you have done better? How can you deepen your connection with your soul mind?

Adaptability: Day 27

MORNING
Experience A, B, C, and D.

A. Meditation

1. *Invitation*

- Rub your palms together briskly for a few seconds.

- Then, rest your hands, palms up, in your lap or on your thighs.

- Make a circle with thumb and forefinger with the remaining fingers relaxed.

- Sit quietly for a few moments, eyes closed.

- With eyes still closed, raise them to focus on an imaginary small dot in the middle of your forehead. Maintain that focus throughout the meditation. Hold a receptive attitude. Do not worry about what it is that you receive.

2. *This Day's Intention*

- When you are ready to shift into making your intention, think to yourself:
  I will focus on the big picture, not just on myself.

- Repeat:
  I will focus on the big picture, not just on myself.

3. *Releasing and Relaxing*

- After a few moments, release your intention and rest in peaceful, receptive inner connection for a minute or two. Release thoughts of past or future that may arise and return to your meditation.

4. *Return*

- When you are ready, take a couple of deep breaths, open your eyes, and bring yourself back to your outer life.

5. *Start the Day*

- With eyes open, say aloud:
  I will focus on the big picture, not just on myself.

B. Quotation

> *Our vision must be broad. We cannot allow our focus on self to keep us from seeing the larger picture. There is always something more to be discovered, always something more to learn.*
>
> —The Lecturer

C. Life Story: *Needless Wonder*

Will and I first met three decades ago. I terrified him by wanting us to get married, so he disappeared off the face of my life for 25 years. When we met again at a bed and breakfast in British Columbia after spending hours each week on the phone for a year, our spark was incandescent. Will has avoided traditional entanglements—including marriage—all his life. So when I came toting a backpack still filled with "normal" expectations, storm warnings went up.

Will lives in the state of Washington. I lived 3,000 miles away in Virginia. I had family, though, in Portland, Oregon. Portland made sense to me—and it was just 300 miles from Will. I packed up and moved my job, my cat, and me.

That first year, I visited Will two or three times, and then engineered a week together at a rustic cabin near Lake Wallowa in northeastern Oregon. I assumed he was willing to take time off—without pay—to be with me. Will doesn't blow up when someone chews on his independence, but he was distant and difficult. He did a lot of sleeping and reading that whole week. Drove me crazy.

When I got back from Wallowa, I was mad. Well, if he wanted to see me, he could take the initiative to drive to Portland. He didn't. Eighteen months later, he was still sitting in Spokane and I spiraled down the rabbit hole.

We still spent hours on the phone every week—and he was often the one who called. I knew he cared. Typical of the way I communicated with men, I didn't ask what was going on. I pulled the plug with a *"Let's be friends and nothing more"* letter. Will misunderstood. He thought I wanted to manipulate him into saying, *"Oh, no, I can't bear not to be lovers anymore."* He was wrong. I had anesthetized my feelings to keep what we had, rather than risk losing it all again.

I thought we had almost the perfect relationship. It was sweet, funny, warm, and loving. It just didn't include any together time. It was, I imagined, like being in love with an inmate in a high-security prison. Someone who gets no visits. Someone who wants no visits. We were able to discuss the most absurd, lofty, or embarrassing topics on the phone—and laugh about them or soar to great heights of mutual learning and teaching. I was deeply satisfied with this relationship, and deeply dissatisfied. I didn't mention my growing belief that only one of us enjoyed our infrequent visits—and it wasn't him.

In the Arts & Entertainment series, *Pride and Prejudice*, Mr. Collins says, *"My Charlotte and I are of one mind."* The camera cuts to Charlotte. Her expression says she has paid a high price—a price she is willing to pay—for him to believe that. I had thought the price I had to pay for love with Will was silence. That turned me into a stuffed owl. I could neither hoot nor fly. Keeping our conversations light, happy, funny, and emotionally dishonest was cooling everything I felt for him.

In the past, I'd grown very little through relationships. If tensions arose, I tried to outwait them. Love with Will was different. He was determined to live free—*and* we had an uncommon connectedness. I liked lots of alone time, too. Well, if we were more than friends, now and then I wanted to *be* more than friends.

Finally, I told him I had become a "needless wonder," someone with no needs except his. Was he open to more frequent visits than a few days at Thanksgiving and a few days over a long weekend during the year? This question may not sound Earth-shaking to you, but it was a first for me in the adaptability area. I was giving him a choice, not making up my mind and telling him how things would be. I was also ready for any response—*"Fine as we are,"* *"Want more visits,"* or *"Want no visits at all."* What mattered was that we were discussing a difficult topic. Whether I got what I wanted was immaterial. This conversation was born of courage, not fear or anger, and that felt *good*.

He thought about it, mumbling, *"Needless wonder?"* A visit each season would work well for him, he responded. *"How else can I see how much you are changing?"* And he smiled. I was not the only person who was adapting. A man who had long recoiled from any predictability in his life outside work was now willing to live with a *plan*.

We would have started getting together four times a year, but the economy tanked. So it's back to twice a year. And because it's understood that it's a cutback based on his finances and mine, I'm fine with that.

When we are together, I'm happy. When we aren't, I'm at peace. Most of my friends find our monogamous, long-distance relationship strange and sparse. If we love each other, how can we bear the separation? For one thing, I don't feel separate from Will. Because our relationship is based on love, not neediness, the rules—such as they are—are different, and they demand a high level of flexibility.

Everything large begins with something small. Everything important starts with something unimportant. Everything we don't like or can't face about ourselves is handed back to us by those we like, by those we dislike, by those we barely know, and especially by those we love. Thus do we fry—and grow—in the crucible of relationship here in Earth School.

D. Growth Practice

- Have you been able to adapt to the needs of love with someone without losing sight of your own needs? If so, how? If not, why not? Do you have a "should" that keeps you from doing this in a way that brings you peace? If so, what is the fear behind it, and the reality?

AFTERNOON

E. Thinking/Journaling

- Write a page in your journal about how much of your life is based on getting others to do something that you think will make you happier. How much of it is based on giving up what's important to you so others will love you?

EVENING

F. Consciousness Expansion

- What do you own that really serves no purpose in your life any more? Could you put it "back in the system" by giving it away or donating it?

G. Think About

In school, we learn everything except what's important—how to connect and stay connected to people we love. Try being kinder or showing more gratitude without any thought of getting something back. Do it just because it's your nature. It is, you know.

√ *Look back. How are you dealing with something that has conquered you many times in the past? Are you beginning to overcome it?*

Good Night Meditation

Relax completely for a few minutes in silence, eyes closed. What did you learn today? What did you share with someone else? What could you have done better? How can you deepen your connection with your soul mind?

Adaptability: Day 28

MORNING
Please work with A, B, C, and D.

A. Meditation

1. *Invitation*

- Rub your palms together briskly for a few seconds.

- Then, rest your hands, palms up, in your lap or on your thighs.

- Make a circle with thumb and forefinger with the remaining fingers relaxed.

- Sit quietly for a few moments, eyes closed.

- With eyes still closed, raise them to focus on an imaginary small dot in the middle of your forehead. Maintain that focus throughout the meditation. Hold a receptive attitude. Do not worry about what it is that you receive.

2. *This Day's Intention*

- When you are ready to shift into making your intention, think to yourself:
I will adapt to unexpected situations.

- Repeat:
I will adapt to unexpected situations.

3. *Releasing and Relaxing*

- After a few moments, release your intention and rest in peaceful, receptive inner connection for a minute or two. Release thoughts of past or future that may arise and return to your meditation.

4. *Return*

- When you are ready, take a couple of deep breaths, open your eyes, and bring yourself back to your outer life.

5. *Start the Day*

- With eyes open, say aloud:
I will adapt to unexpected situations.

B. Quotation

> The art of adaptability is learned by consciously choosing a different response when unexpected things interrupt our schedule or whatever we are doing. The outer mind is displeased at such interruptions. We can take a quick moment of connection with the soul mind, an instant's meditation, and adapt. When we do, we save ourselves much confusion and distress, and we are better prepared to deal with the next unexpected situation. For surely there will be one, and another, to deal with. The art of adaptability is truly an art.
>
> —The Lecturer

C. Life Story: Aurora

At a Portland party two years ago, I met a member of the 100-woman Aurora Chorus. When she played a performance CD for me, it was so beautiful I wanted to audition. *"But,"* I said, *"I don't read music."*

She laughed. *"Many of us don't read a note. If you can carry a tune, you're in."*

I had joined two choirs in my life—always as a soprano because I could take the melody. Here, I was a Soprano Two Mezzo—whatever that was. My line of music was harmony—stuck in the middle somewhere between Soprano Ones, Soprano Twos, Alto Mezzos, Alto Ones, and Alto Twos.

Every now and then, we S2Ms, as we were known, got the melody. About 95% of the time, however, I had to figure out where my notes were among the highly complex, undulating, constantly changing music lines. Joan, our artistic director, loved syncopation, weird rhythms, and songs in foreign languages—especially foreign languages that none of us spoke. Every note, every moment, was a climb up a rock wall. I had hoped that the music would "just come." It didn't. Only after I began putting in ten hard hours a week did it "just come."

Early on, I considered quitting—*strongly* considered it. Who was I to think I would master this music? Who was the director to choose such impossible songs? Why wouldn't she let us bring our music onstage? What had I gotten myself into? Other newbies had already walked out. I could, too. I didn't have to give up all my free time just to feel incompetent. My outer mind was right in there slugging, filling me with doubt and the fear that I could not do this work no matter how hard I stretched. On one outer mind-noisy day, I made a decision to stick with it because the music was powerful, because I had so rarely stuck with *anything*, and because I wanted to be able to look back and say I had accomplished the impossible.

As we got closer to the date of performance, something unexpected happened. We would be practicing a portion of a song and suddenly, all six lines of music would perfectly converge to set up a pure, bell-like harmony that made the bones of my head resonate with beauty.

Once, during a rehearsal, our pianist tried to bolster our confidence after we'd done a particularly tune-confused job with a song. She told us about a singer who gave a one-woman concert, and then angrily strode off stage, complaining bitterly that she had never sung more badly.

"That singer was upset," Signe said, *"but the rest of us—the listeners—were in tears at how beautiful, how glorious her singing had been. The music you sing,"* she added, *"is not for you. The singers never get to hear the best part. That's reserved for the audience. It is your gift to them."*

I was sure she was right. I also knew how it felt to be rung like a tuning fork—an experience only someone in the middle of it all could possibly have.

I sang with Aurora for a full year—for two concerts—and then quit to write this book. I couldn't do both. I still miss it. I miss the music and the community and the gift we freely offered to each other and to friends and strangers.

A poem about Aurora poured out of me. It described what it was like to calm my doubts and fears, reach *way* down deep, and give it all I had.

> *Goosebumps racing head to toe,*
> *Tears filling my eyes,*
> *Now I know why we sing what we sing.*
> *It's all perfect.*
> *Now I know where I fit,*
> *Imperfect as I am.*
> *If I'm willing to work,*

To do what doesn't come easily,
I can help create a day unlike any other.
A day colored with all that we are—the music
And what we give of ourselves
In the spaces between the notes.

We are the peaceful weavers
Of a singing community.
If I, one of the newest, weakest threads
In this quilt of singers
Should break,
They would know it.

The loss would shiver across their heart,
Which has somehow—I don't know how—
Become our heart.

All of us, like Icarus,
Fly to the sun of song on wings of wax
That melt, and throw us into the fire,
Burning away the soft parts,
Leaving behind the strong parts,
So we can make them stronger still.

So we can stand side by side,
In purple scarves, laughing and
Singing, "We are Aurora.
Hear us roar!"

D. Growth Practice

- Watch any tendencies to feel doubtful or fearful today. Weigh them in a conscious light. Reach out. Ask someone to join you for a walk in a park—or if you don't have a park nearby, walk along an area that has some trees. Or find one tree to appreciate.

AFTERNOON

E. Thinking/Journaling

- Describe an experience that has made you stronger as a person.

EVENING

F. Consciousness Expansion

- Consider using great music, art, or literature to help you live in the moment. Just as pain carves out space in us that can be filled with compassion, what if music, art, and literature are ways to link heart and mind, enriching both in the process?

G. Think About

We are moved to find a sense of purpose. Many who look for their "mission" are hoping for something grand, something worthy of public celebration. Aren't our lives bursting with opportunities to connect in ways that will be appreciated by those on the receiving end? If those acts can be used as a measurement of how well we fulfill our mission in life, can we not all start there? Now? In this moment?

Good Night Meditation

Relax completely for a few minutes in silence, eyes closed. What did you learn today? What did you share with someone else? What could you have done better? How can you deepen your connection with your soul mind?

Afterword
Everything Matters

The most interesting period of your life is now. Make every moment count. Enjoy the good things that come to you as a result of your positive actions. Do not condemn. Do not speak idly against mankind, groups, or even government. Don't weigh yourself down by worrying and fretting. Don't focus on what you think might happen or on what someone else said. Don't speak or act negatively and don't be swayed by someone else's negative thoughts or actions. Do not worry about what others do.

You can spoil the beauty of your days with worry over others' actions, over the economy, over anything that happens in society or in the world. You have better things, much better things to do with your life. Do those things. Do them now.

-The Lecturer

Much of my life could be called inconsequential if "consequential" means making a real effort to grow and contribute to the world around me. I didn't want to work at it—even though I, more than most, knew that there was work to be done.

I've made enough strides in the past few years that even if I got mashed flat by a bus tomorrow, I'd be okay with it. I'd better be okay. I have no choice about that part. We all die.

The lecturer spoke of the life review—a brief period just before we pass over. All the main events flash before us, he said, together with emotions—not *our* emotions but those felt by the people whose lives we touched and changed for good, or not so good. I don't know about the life you've lived, but without this work, my life review would have been dark and tormented, indeed.

I can't go back and fix what I broke. I can't relive any of it. I can't change the choices made and the wheels put into motion because of them. I used to say I regretted nothing. That's because I ignored the past. What's the use of looking back, right? Now I know that if we don't look back, we don't learn from the past. We do repeat it—repeatedly.

Many believe life's mostly about getting, with a little giving thrown in as an afterthought. The truth is that life's about making a consistent effort to morph into someone better than we started out as.

The lecturer said that we never become so advanced that we can run around "acting spiritual," pretending that nothing really matters. *Everything* matters. That's why we're here. We become conscious so we can really live and do the work for which we were created. Our great work is to learn how to partner with the inner Self, to light our small candle at that inner fire—and to pay it forward by interacting with compassion and understanding toward those we meet.

It's all just experience, that's true. And yet, as the lecturer said, it's experience with purpose. Through our connections, we learn why we are here—to consciously live as one in peace, joy, and love.

And for those who worry that living in the now will always be a terrific struggle, here's a nugget of hope. The more conscious we become, the more natural it feels to live consciously. Don't just take my word for it. In his book, *The Brain that Changes Itself,* Norman Doidge, MD, talks about neuroplasticity. One of the most thrilling concepts ever to come out of science lies in that six-syllable word.

We've all heard that thoughts are things and by changing our minds, we can change our lives. Well, science has finally caught up. Neuroplasticity refers to the scientifically proven ability of the brain to change both its structure and function—through thinking. So there it is. We remodel our brains as we move through the world with an attitude of patience, perseverance, and adaptability. Science now agrees that we evolve through learning, growing, and expanding in consciousness.

That's not bad for creatures that only yesterday crawled out of the ocean and onto the beach. Not bad for folks who started out with dim thoughts about dinner, thoughts that are shifting to, *"What are we doing here, anyway?"*

About the Author

Carol Marleigh Kline edits the online *Journal of the American Chiropractic Association (JACA Online)*. A former television talk show host, anchor, and producer, she coordinated Smithsonian Resident Associates' programs and taught broadcast journalism at UNC/ Greensboro and Wake Forest.

Carol graduated from the University of Southern California and earned an M.A. at Columbia University. She's listed in *Who's Who of American Women*.

INDEX

Available from NorlightsPress and
fine booksellers everywhere

Toll free: 888-558-4354   **Online:** www.norlightspress.com

Shipping Info:
Add $2.95 for first item and $1.00 for each additional item

Name _____

Address _____

Daytime Phone _____

E-mail _____

No. Copies	Title	Price (each)	Total Cost

Subtotal	
Shipping	
Total	

Payment by (circle one):
Check   Visa   Mastercard   Discover   Am Express

Card number_____3 digit code_____

Exp.date_____ Signature_____

Mailing Address:
2721 Tulip Tree Rd.
Nashville, IN 47448

Sign up to receive our catalogue at
www.norlightspress.com

CPSIA information can be obtained at www.ICGtesting.com

233762LV00002B/148/P